THE
BELL
NOTES

Also by Arthur M. Young

THE REFLEXIVE UNIVERSE
Evolution of Consciousness

THE GEOMETRY OF MEANING

Arthur M.Young

THE
BELL
NOTES

A Journey from

Physics to Metaphysics

Arthur M. Young

A Merloyd Lawrence Book
DELACORTE PRESS/SEYMOUR LAWRENCE

A Merloyd Lawrence Book
Published by
Delacorte Press/Seymour Lawrence
1 Dag Hammarskjold Plaza
New York, N.Y. 10017

ACKNOWLEDGMENTS

Grateful acknowledgment is made for permission to use the following copyrighted material.

From *Tibetan Yoga and Secret Doctrines* by W. Y. Evans-Wentz: Copyright © 1958 by W. Y. Evans-Wentz. Reprinted by permission of Oxford University Press, Inc.

From COLLECTED POEMS AND PLAYS by Rabindranath Tagore: "Fruit Gathering" #29, and "Stray Birds" #16 copyright 1916 by Macmillan Publishing Co., Inc., renewed 1944 by Rabindranath Tagore. "Crossing" #42 copyright 1918 by Macmillan Publishing Co., Inc., renewed 1946 by Rabindranath Tagore. Reprinted with permission of Macmillan Publishing Co., Inc., the Trustees of the Tagore Estate, and Macmillan, London and Basingstoke.

From ESSAYS IN ZEN BUDDHISM by D. T. Suzuki: Reprinted by permission of Grove Press, Inc. All rights reserved. Used by permission of the Hutchinson Publishing Group.

Manufactured in the United States of America

First printing

Designed by Laura Bernay

LIBRARY OF CONGRESS CATALOGING IN PUBLICATION DATA

Young, Arthur M 1905–
  The Bell notes.

  "A Merloyd Lawrence book."
  Includes index.
  1. Young, Arthur M., 1905– 2. Helicopters—
History. 3. Metaphysics. I. Title.
TL540.Y64A33   191 [B]   78-20802
ISBN 0-440-00550-7 (hardcover)
ISBN 0-440-00551-5 (paperback)

Acknowledgments

The idea of sifting through my journal for a readable typescript owes its origin to Isabel Bayley, who in 1946 and 1947 made the first compilation. At this time we divided the material into several headings, "Bell Notes," "Pensées," "Painting," and "Yoga." As the years passed, I came to realize that this separation into categories was artificial and obliterated essential connections. In which category would dreams of the future be placed? Yet these dreams were a powerful stimulus to my interest in a more comprehensive cosmology. So I dispensed with categories and eventually, with the encouragement of Ira Einhorn, got all six volumes typed in chronological order.

Now it was too long; drastic cutting was necessary. Here again I depended on friends, Nancy Kleban, my wife Ruth, and most of all on my editor, Merloyd Lawrence.

THE BELL NOTES
is published by arrangement with
Robert Briggs Associates,
San Francisco

Contents

The publishers wish to thank Sheila La Farge for her assistance in preparing this book for publication.

To LARRY BELL, for making the helicopter possible

To BART KELLEY, for assisting throughout and for carrying the torch since 1947

And to RUTH, for becoming my wife and partner in my new life and search into the unknown

FOREWORD

It is remarkable that at the very moment of his greatest technological triumph, Arthur Young was readying for a total change of course. Success, to him, was not so much a terminus as the signal for a necessary and welcome transition—of which these "Bell Notes" are the vivid record. On March 8, 1946, Young's machine, the Bell Model 47, was awarded the world's first commercial helicopter license. It was the culmination of almost eighteen years' work. By then, however, he had come to see the helicopter chiefly as a metaphor for the evolving spirit—the winged self which he now began to call the "psychopter."

Young's renewed ambition "to find and name the laws of the mind, which are the laws of reality" would have daunted a lesser man. His efforts while at Princeton to develop a "theory of structure and process" had led nowhere. Relativity theory and the mathematical logic of Bertrand Russell, which had then absorbed him, now seemed increasingly sterile. ("Russell, who once through mutual friends chanced to come to my house in Paoli, and whom I cornered in order to explain my solution to the paradoxes he had bequeathed posterity, hastened to assure me that he was no longer interested in mathematics, he had transferred his attentions to women.") And while the atomic bombs dropped on Hiroshima and Nagasaki in 1945 underscored the urgent need for a new spiritual and moral order, philosophy and science alike appeared to have turned their backs on the transcendent world.

As an inventor Young had gotten into the habit of making a chronological record of ideas and tests, primarily for patent purposes. At first he had kept a series of notebooks by subject, but as time went on he found that a single diary was preferable, because connections not immediately apparent were likely to come to light later. This journal became a focus for his thinking.

("There is a sort of self-reinforcement, like a laser beam," he observes.) From 1939 on, he kept all notes chronologically in one series of diaries, which continues up to the present day. In the entries reproduced here, dating from October 1945 to November 1947, we follow his progress in perhaps the most crucial period of his career as he wrestles simultaneously with the problems of the helicopter, the paradoxes of Zen, Jungian dream analysis, the arduous discipline of Hatha Yoga, and the looming challenge of the psychopter to which all this was prelude.

He became an explorer of the wilder reaches of mind. In a helicopter accident he had experienced the odd sensation of being "out of the body." (He remembers seeing himself roll over when the helicopter overturned.) Impressed by J. W. Dunne's book *An Experiment with Time,* he trained himself to use hypnagogic images, and discovered that he had precognitive dreams too. In April 1947 we find him speculating about means of photographing the human aura—the process which later became famous as Kirlian photography. Later that same month he had a meeting at the Ritz Hotel in New York with the talented psychic Eileen Garrett, who gave him a "reading" that left him dumbfounded.

During the next five years (a time he now refers to as his "Gee Whiz!" period), he systematically investigated the so-called "psi" phenomena which the scientific establishment swept under the rug. What was needed, he came to realize, was some sort of "unified field theory" of consciousness, in the absence of which there was little hope of integrating the accumulating chaos of data turned up by the parapsychologists. (Unless you have a hypothesis, he points out, you cannot even know whether you have changed your mind.) A good part of his success with the helicopter, he felt, could be attributed to the "Gardenville group" of co-workers he had gathered about him at Buffalo, N.Y. It was natural, therefore, that he should look for collaborators, and in 1952 set up the Foundation for the Study of Consciousness in Philadelphia. But because there was no paradigm on which to focus group work, he set about to develop one which would account for life and consciousness. This resulted in two books, *The Reflexive Universe* and *The Geometry of Meaning.* With their completion he set up the Institute for the

Study of Consciousness in Berkeley, whose purpose is to teach the theory and encourage its development and use, both in research and educational reform.

Meanwhile the path he had chosen led steadily away from conventional determinism. Among the many influences of the period covered by the "Bell Notes," for example, are the seventeenth-century German shoemaker-mystic Jakob Boehme; Charles Fort, the American critic of science, who gleefully compiled data which confounded orthodoxy; Mme. H. P. Blavatsky, founder of the Theosophical Society; Indian scientist Sir Jagadis Chandra Bose, best known for his controversial work on the sensitivities of plants; and the anonymous medieval author of *The Cloud of Unknowing,* which Young thought one of the most profound writings ever to come out of the West.

But if the message of the mystics was that the way to enlightenment lay through love rather than logic—and it was a teaching he fully accepted—Young continued to assert the uses of reason. "Regardless of the limitations of consciousness and of words," he says, "they *are* what we have to deal with." In the process of becoming a metaphysician, the inventor did not abandon his practicality. "To be free of the laws we must know what they are. That is the role of consciousness," he asserts confidently. Quantum mechanics and astrology proved equally absorbing, and might perhaps have more to do with each other than their respective adherents grasped. If he studied the *Gita,* he also read Eddington and Schrödinger. For him *mythos* and *logos* comprised one seamless web. Any attempt to advance the claims of the one at the expense of the other was as foolish as it was futile. "To find out about a thing is humbly to learn the shape of nature which is also the will of God," he observes. (Cf. Spinoza's "The more we know of particular things, the more we know of God.")

It was in quantum physics above all, however, that he found the basis for his new paradigm of reality (described in his books *The Reflexive Universe* and *The Geometry of Meaning*). He came to perceive that the "uncertainty" discovered by Heisenberg, and demonstrated to be fundamental to the behavior of atomic particles, can be equated with freedom, placing a definite limit on determinism as a means of understanding the universe. While physicists evolve ever more complex explanations, Young argues

that the unpredictability of nuclear particles is an indication
that we have reached the realm of action rather than of things,
and that such unpredictability will never be "overcome." In
other words, the uncertainty of the electron must be seen as
ontological, and not simply as epistemological. The quantum of
action (the photon or fundamental unit of light) cannot be
comprehended in terms of space and time. In fact, it is from the
photon, from light, that mass, energy, and time are born, and it
must therefore be recognized as "first cause"—which is precisely
the teaching of revealed religion.

The indeterminacy which is confusing the physicists should,
Young contends, be regarded as a great and positive discovery,
disclosing an order of which we are a part, more basic than the
material universe. To the determinist mind, ruled by the iron
law of entropy, the inevitable end of men and stars alike is a
thin gruel of atoms evenly distributed through space: uniform
mass at a uniform temperature very little above absolute zero. In
charting the process of cosmic evolution, Arthur Young rejects
this dismal and absurd vision. He provides a formal basis for
integrating the laws of science with both empirical facts and the
ancient religious beliefs to which much of humankind adheres.
The pages which follow describe the first tentative steps of a
spiritual and intellectual pilgrimage which is perhaps without
modern parallel.

PETER DREYER

INTRODUCTION:

The Making of
a Helicopter

On the evening of September 3, 1941, I went to the Bell Aircraft Company in Buffalo. In a suitcase I carried a remote control model helicopter, the fruit of almost twelve years of research on the problem of vertical flight.

My interest in the helicopter started in 1928. I had gone to Washington to the Patent Office to evaluate various ideas I'd had for inventions. If I could find some practical problem to work on for the next ten to fifteen years, I could return to my study of philosophy and the theory of process later with a better grasp of how things work. (This other search is described in my book *The Reflexive Universe.*) The idea that did impress me was not suggested by the Patent Office. It was in a small book by Anton Flettner, the inventor of the boat propelled by rotating cylinders which had crossed the Atlantic in 1927.

Flettner showed a picture of a huge windmill with small propellers, themselves windmills, at the tips. The wind turns the big windmill which in turn makes the small propellers rotate at high speed, requiring smaller gears to pick up the power.

When I went to bed that night I saw Flettner's idea applied to a helicopter. A large rotor propelled by small propellers at the blade tips would not only not require heavy gearing but it would solve the "torque problem," *i.e.,* how to counteract the twist resulting from turning the large rotor.

As I was to learn in the years following, on my periodic trips to libraries in Washington, Detroit, and other cities, there had been many attempts to build helicopters since the early 1900s. Leonardo had of course made sketches, but he had not shown any way of correcting the torque. Furthermore, not until the coming of the automobile with its internal combustion engine was it possible to obtain engines sufficiently powerful and light enough even to approach the requirements of vertical flight. Indeed, the smaller power requirements of the airplane were largely responsible for the fact that the airplane succeeded first. Certainly there were many more attempts to make helicopters than airplanes in those early days.

Among others, D'Ascanio and Isacco in Italy, Pescara in Spain, Karman and Petroczy in Austria, Berliner and Cooper-Hewitt in the U.S., and Oemichen and Breguet in France, made helicopters. Both Oemichen and Breguet succeeded on actual flights over a kilometer closed circuit, but at speeds of the order of 6 miles per hour. Not until 1937, some nine years after I started, did Focke, a German airplane designer, succeed in building a helicopter which obtained an average speed of sixty-eight miles per hour. And it was soon after this (as far as I know) that Sikorsky, who had first attempted a helicopter in 1909, and then become the successful designer of large airplanes, returned to the helicopter and achieved in 1938 the first truly successful experimental flights in the U.S. By May of 1942 a larger Sikorsky machine, the famous XR4, flew to Dayton, Ohio, for delivery to the Air Force.

But in 1928, despite advances in engine design, there were still no successful helicopters. In fact, there was no agreement as to design. Some used coaxial rotors (two rotors turning in opposite directions on the same shaft). Some used side by side rotors; some had four lifting rotors. Oemichen made over 1,000 flights in a machine with four lifting rotors and nine auxiliary propellers. There was even one design in the form of a maple seed. And, as I later learned, Isacco had a large single rotor turned by propellers and engines on the ends of the blades.

In any case, in 1928 the helicopter was an interesting challenge and I was intrigued by the possibility suggested by Flettner's design for a large windmill, of a single rotor with propellers at the tips.

I went back to Radnor, Pennsylvania, with the determination to try this idea. At a toy store I found rubber bands, carved wooden propellers, light balsa wood strips, Japanese silk, and dope (lacquer) and soon had made a model helicopter, about six feet in diameter.

It flew nicely but with short duration, indicating that a helicopter would require more power than an airplane.

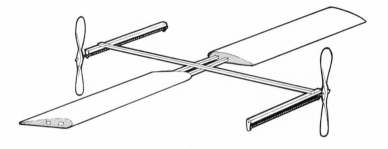

First model

For the next nine years I struggled with this design. During the first phase of the work I developed the use of models powered by electric motors (the model technique became important later). During this period the most significant development was a whirling arm with which I could make accurate tests of propeller efficiency. I also built equipment to measure the lift and horsepower of the electric model and discovered the formulas to predict lift and horsepower for full scale.

I next undertook a larger machine. Since I had neither facilities nor finances for a full-scale model, I decided on an intermediate 20-horsepower machine, which I purposely made small in order to achieve high power density. Because this would increase the stresses to values even greater than with full scale, and do so within a small compass, it would be an ideal test vehicle. I anticipated that I would use remote control to fly it.

The stresses were even larger than I anticipated. On its first test the propeller blades broke off. The stress induced by rotating the small propellers at 4,000 rpm and at the same time having to reverse the direction of their rotation as the big rotor turned 400 times per minute was too much.

I built stronger blades. The second time the whole shaft broke off and the machine destroyed itself.

A third time I rebuilt everything using forged magnesium alloy blades and nickel vanadium steel shafts designed for maximum strength. It held up. Next came the overspeed test with lift wing blades at flat pitch (no lift). This time it blew up with a vengeance.

These explorations, in which I never even got to the question of flight, were very time-consuming but provided valuable experience, both in calculating stress and redesigning and building parts. It was now 1938 and I had bought an old farm in Paoli. I rebuilt the barn into a shop and test area for model flights. I was beginning to think I should turn to a simpler configuration when I attended the first of the Rotating Wing Aircraft meetings, organized by Burke Wilford. There I saw Sikorsky's film and was impressed with his argument for correcting the torque by means of a tail rotor.

I also heard a paper by Platt, in which he argued that a rotor with blades hinged to the mast would be stable in flight because the body could swing without tilting the rotor. This was the argument given in *Le Vol Vertical,* a French text on helicopters, but it was not until I heard it from Platt that I questioned it. Would the hinged rotor not follow the inclined mast? And was it stable in flight?

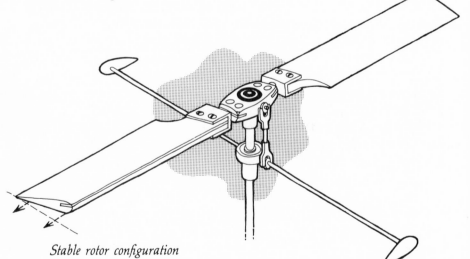

Stable rotor configuration

I went back to my shop and built a small electric model to test a hinged rotor. Tipping the mast with the rotor turning, I could see the rotor immediately "follow" the mast so that, despite the articulation, the rotor remained perpendicular to the mast. In flight it was definitely unstable, tipping as it took off and dashing in the direction of the tip, only to swing back and reverse direction. After several swings of increasing amplitude, it would upset.

The problem of obtaining a rotor system that would provide stable flight now took my attention. Since the hinged rotor, first proposed by Breguet in 1907, was used by many pioneers, including the Frenchman Oemichen whose work I especially admired, was it not possible that its unstable flight was responsible for their lack of success? (Oemichen had ended by attaching a balloon to his helicopter, not for lift but for stability.) Was it not likely that some of the wrecks which terminated helicopter flights in the past were due to this factor?

I could now put my mechanical skills to work. My long apprenticeship had taught me the virtue of simplicity, and returning to small models I could give my attention to principles and especially to stability. I could concentrate on flight. If the model were wrecked, I could rebuild it in a day or so and carry on. In this way I was able to speed up the process of trial and error, to make mistakes and learn from them, with a minimum of time invested. So after a half dozen different rotor configurations, I hit upon the device of using a stabilizer bar linked directly to the rotor. In this way the rotor plane was controlled independently of the mast, which was attached to the rotor hub by a universal joint.

This configuration had superb stability. It could hover indefinitely without moving. It was no problem now to add remote control. With the remote control I could fly it around a prescribed course in the interior of the old barn, or even fly it out the barn door and back.

It was the description of this model given by a friend to engineers at Bell Aircraft Company that resulted in my being invited to come there and give a demonstration.

Which brings me to September 1941. At the gate of the Bell Aircraft Company the guard checked with the engineer who had invited me and I was permitted to enter. I was escorted to the factory where I unpacked the model and flew it in the rather cramped space between the Airacobra pursuit planes which filled most of the space in the factory.

By this time a number of engineers were gathered. We adjourned to the projection room where I showed my film "Principles of Stability" which, starting with an unstable model, demonstrated the flight of different types of rotors I'd used, ending with the remote control model I'd just flown in the plant.

Bell's patent attorney then informed me that Bell would like to make an arrangement. I was introduced to Larry Bell himself, whom I liked from the first. In November of that year we signed a contract, I to assign my helicopter patents to Bell and Bell to build two helicopters. (I insisted on two in case the first was wrecked.) I asked if my assistant, Bart Kelley, could come too and was told yes, if he could work for $36 a week, a small sum even in those days.

Bart Kelley, whom I'd known since boyhood, had worked with me on models back in the summer of 1931. He had then disappeared, to return again one summer night in 1941, just at a time when I could use his help. He remained during the rest of the summer, assisting me and teaching himself how helicopters were made. When I told him Bell's offer, he accepted. (Bart worked with me and remained after I left, becoming Vice President in charge of engineering. He is now officially retired but still plays an active part in the company.)

Now that I'd joined Bell I assumed that the organization would take over my responsibilities and build the two helicopters, but, as I gradually came to be aware, nothing happened and nothing would happen. The company, already seething with wartime activity, working three shifts and expanding all the time, hardly seemed to know of my existence, much less how to build helicopters. But I did not realize the extent of my predicament until after about two months of waiting around. An engineer who had been assigned to me showed me the budget he was working on—$250,000. I thought fair enough, but to my consternation I found it was not to build two helicopters, as the contract had specified, but to *draw* the helicopters.

This was the normal procedure for airplanes, which required elaborate drawings to make the precisely curved metal panels of which body and wings consisted. It would hardly do for the complex mechanism of the helicopter, involving all kinds of hitherto untried mechanisms. I wanted to build the helicopters first with working drawings only and get them to fly. Then, when we knew the requirements, we could make the drawings for the production prototype.

This woke me up to the fact that I'd have to act myself. I went to Russ Creighton, head of production at the factory, and explained my predicament. He spoke my language and understood. He agreed to sign a budget which provided for *building* two helicopters for $250,000. Then he added a provision: "provided only that the engineering [drafting] department had nothing to do with it."

But even with the budget question set to right, the problem remained. How to get something built? In my former life at Paoli, I could plan a model, go over to the barn, build it and fly it, but I never even thought about full scale. How to begin? I went over to my temporary shop in the factory, mocked up an engine and, twenty feet away, a tail rotor. How would I ever fill the space between with actual machinery that would lift 2,000 pounds into the air? The problem seemed insurmountable. There was nothing to do but make everything six times model size. Drawings would be straightforward but making the parts would require machinery and machinists. Assembly and flight would require space. We would have to have a plant of our own. Further, the project, small as it now was, was already split into office, model shop, and drafting room, each in a different location. It would be far better to get the project all in one place for better coordination. Then with a machine shop and space to build and fly helicopters, we would be in business.

I issued a memorandum stating the need for a plant of our own. When this brought no result I engaged a real estate company in Buffalo to look for a suitable place.

Things were now beginning to take shape. With the help of my shop in the factory, I was able to build a final model involving a control system that would be suited to pilot operation. (The remote control model system did not lend itself to pilot operation.) The all-important gears were being made. But still something was holding us back; funds were not released. At last I learned why. L. Bell wanted to see a model demonstration of safe descent in case of engine failure.

This was difficult in the space available. So I arranged a vertical wire and had the model climb up it some thirty feet to the ceiling, then cut the power and let it descend in auto-rotation. When it was ready, I went to the restaurant where Larry had lunch and told him it would be ready when he returned. I obtained two raw eggs from the chef. Back at the shop I placed one egg on the model and put it through the test. Unfortunately, the model climbed too fast and the egg bounced off when it hit the ceiling. Then Larry came. I was more careful this time. The model climbed to the ceiling; I cut the power; it descended without breaking the egg. Larry was delighted.

After that funds were released and the property we had found most suitable was leased. This was a garage on the outskirts of Buffalo, with open space behind it, a former Chrysler Agency. The maintenance department got to work, surrounded it with a board fence painted Navy gray, floodlights, and an armed guard. I commented that this strategy only called attention to it, so the floodlights were removed and the guard reduced to a single night watchman.

On June 23, 1942, we moved to the new location. Gardenville, as it came to be called, was ideal for our purpose. Behind the building proper was a good-size yard where we would do the preliminary testing—beyond that an open meadow, suitable for short flights. The building itself was divided into four parts: 1. an office space with desks for myself and my "brain trust" (B. Kelley, Tom Harriman, and Charlie Seibel; the secretary, Mary McCann; and later, the pilot, Floyd Carlson); 2. the machine shop and assembly area, which occupied more than half the total space; 3. the wood shop for making blades; 4. the drafting room where drawings were made, later referred to as the paper shop. What had been a display room for Chryslers was set aside as a model shop.

The helicopter project was now augmented by flight mechanics, body men, a welder, and two patternmakers (for the wood shop) plus Tom Darner, the youth whom I'd taught to make blades before I came to Bell. We were also fortunate in the addition of three of the best toolmakers from the Bell factory, who had somehow got wind of the operation and applied for transfer. The paper shop now included five men.

We could now get to work in earnest and Model 30, our first helicopter, was underway. Draftsmen made drawings; machinists made masts, rotor hub, and control system; patternmakers made wooden blades (actually a composite of steel-impregnated fir and balsa). The body men and the welder made the fuselage and landing gear. The riveted magnesium tail boom was made in the main plant to drawings.

About six months after we came to Gardenville we had a helicopter ready to be wheeled out, with long legs of 3-inch dural tubing, a 32-foot rotor, and a 160 horsepower Franklin air-cooled engine. (All dimensions were six times those of the model.)

But Model 30, its Bell number, or Genevieve, as it was christened when we first took it out December 1942, was a bit cumbersome. To get it out the door, the legs had to be removed, then it was wheeled out on a dolly, and pushed up a ramp so that the legs could be replaced. By this time everyone was frozen stiff, as was the engine, which had the additional handicap of having to push the huge rotor, for at this stage we had no clutch. A storage battery for starting was wheeled out on an express wagon, but the starter was unequal to the task. My solution was simple: use two batteries (24 volts). This did the trick, and I actually believe caused less strain on the motor because it turned over fast and didn't draw as much current.

Since I was not a pilot, and had never even flown an airplane,

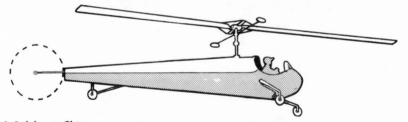

Model 30 Ship 1

much less a helicopter, my first hops were brief and erratic, six inches or a foot at most. I did not fly it long. We were assigned a regular pilot, Floyd Carlson, who is still with the company.

We now began to encounter the problems of helicopters, problems that are not apparent until flights are attempted, and which had caused the demise of many pioneers before us. (I later learned that by 1943 there had been 343 helicopter companies that had failed.)

To appreciate these problems, which cost us several crack-ups with the necessity of rebuilding and making design changes, it would be necessary to go into a lot of technical detail which would only tax the patience of the lay reader. Suffice it to say, thanks to the flexibility of the Gardenville group, which could work in a coordinated way with a minimum of red tape, we were able to take these problems in our stride, so that by July 1943 we had Ship 1 flying well up to speeds in excess of 70 miles per hour. Then, due to an unsuitable landing gear, this ship was damaged on a power-off landing.

Meanwhile Ship 2, a streamlined two-passenger version, became our test vehicle. The first ship was rebuilt with a raised tail rotor and landing gear modified to permit the machine to remain in the tipped-back position for the touchdown in power-off landings.

Then came the problem of engine wear, which plagued our early efforts. The cause of this was traced to gear wear, which was in turn corrected.

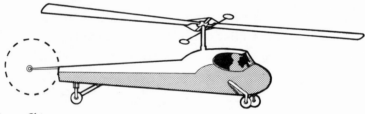

Model 30 Ship 2

Next, we started giving rides to visitors and the helicopter was tried out on rescue missions. Larry Bell had his ride. The time had come for the helicopter to make its debut. It was given a two-page spread in the Sunday paper, with the consequence that the traffic on the road behind our shop, which before had paid no attention to our test flights, was now blocked with spectators.

Then came a flight indoors in the Buffalo Armory. The pilot, despite the glare of searchlights, maneuvered the ship slowly around under perfect control, ending by bringing the front wheel into my extended hand.

Later, on July 4, 1944, Ship 1 was flying again and gave a demonstration to a crowd of 5,000 in the Buffalo Stadium.

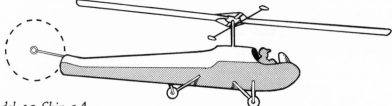

Model 30 Ship 1A

At about this time Larry Bell, foreseeing the time when pursuit airplanes could no longer be sold, sent a contingent of engineers from the main engineering department to Gardenville to learn about helicopters. The plan was to design a large ship, Model 42, which, according to a market survey, would better meet demand. (It was anticipated that helicopters would be used to carry passengers to airports.)

Here began the problem that was later to become important, and which is the main theme of the "Bell Notes," a difference of philosophy. At Gardenville, we built things, tested them, modified them until they worked, and *then* made the drawings. The main engineering group made drawings, sent them to the plant, and only the project engineer ever saw the product fly. This was successful with airplanes because the airplane did not involve unknowns; these had been ironed out in the forty years of development since the Wright Brothers. In retrospect, I can only suppose that Larry, who did indeed appreciate the problems and the Gardenville way of dealing with them, still felt that, with the basics having been established, the main engineering department could do the job better. Besides, he had to think of what was in the best interests of the company, which, with its thousands of employees, would be out of work when the war ended.

Meanwhile, we, the Gardenville group, were still not satisfied with Ships 1 and 2. In early 1945 we started on Ship 3, which was to incorporate the best we had found in our experience so far. A four-wheeled landing gear was designed which provided a better behaved takeoff. A different body shape, with instrument panel in the middle and almost no floor, gave unobstructed vertical vision. And later a bubble canopy, blown from heated Plexiglas like a soap bubble, gave undistorted vision.

This ship, launched on April 20, 1945, was an immediate success. With room for two passengers, no body or windshield, only a small instrument column between passenger and pilot, one had an unobstructed view up and down. It was like sitting in a chair and flying about through space. Vice President Truman had witnessed flights a few weeks before we started giving rides. I recall his smile as we stood together waiting for it to take off. Now we were giving rides to whoever came by— Governor Dewey, Mayor LaGuardia. (I recall the somewhat ludicrous sight of the latter, already short, stooping as he ran out under the rotor.) Hundreds at the plant also had rides, and it improved morale, not only for our own group but for others who might have been depressed by the demise of the pursuit airplane.

Model 30 Ship 3

Then came the great blow. Since we were now successful, we were to be transported back to the main plant. This had now been moved to Niagara Falls, the Wheatfield Plant, built and owned by the government and on the edge of a commodious airport.

We were moved, machinery and all, June 24th, exactly three years after we had moved to Gardenville. We were installed in a hangar: office, paper shop, machine shop, wood shop, and model shop, partitioned off as before with plywood walls.

The most critical time had come; the drawings for Model 47, the production prototype, had to be made. The drafting department sent us more men, but they were not their best and made so many mistakes I recall saying to Bart it would be better to buy the drawings from Sears Roebuck and fill in the dimensions ourselves. And I really exerted myself to get everything just right. Mast, hub, blade grips, bar control system, transmission with ground gears, all were done over to incorporate our experience and the opportunity to use forgings and take advantage of mass production.

What made it more difficult was that at this time Bart was sent to Germany to learn what they had to offer in helicopters.

But luck was with us and on December 8, 1945, less than six months after we came to Wheatfield, the first Model 47 was rolled out, complete with bubble canopy. It was the first Bell ship, I was told, to be completed on schedule. We had even better lift than anticipated, which made for a very good performance, even with two passengers. I have a photo of Model 47 hovering with seven people hanging on to it.

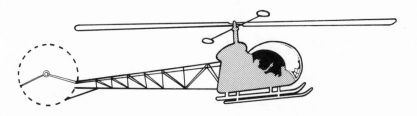

Model 47

This ship was one of ten made from production parts but assembled by our own crew as a transition to the full production ship, which was to come off the assembly line. This ultimately turned out to be a fiasco; it took twice as long to assemble it with an assembly line.

This brings me to the time when I began what I call the "Bell Notes."

It had been my custom since I started on the helicopter to keep a journal in which I sketched my ideas and noted results and dates. This was important not only for patents, but also, by encouraging a sort of inner debate, for providing a stimulus to new ideas. When the helicopter was ready for production, changes and inventions had to cease and the momentum of my inner discourse took a different direction. My writing became introspective and philosophical.

These notes were not so much about the helicopter as they were an emotional outlet for my frustrations during the transition, as the main plant took over the job of building helicopters. They were also notes on the "psychopter," which I began to realize was my true interest.

For two reasons the notes should not be taken as a criticism of Bell. In the first place, they present only my side of the story. In the second place, Bell Aircraft did undergo a transformation. Eventually the seed of Gardenville did create a new entity—Bell Helicopter Company, now located in Texas.

It is important to mention that just prior to the launching of Model 47, shaken by the atom bomb (1945), anticipating that my task would be ended in about a year, and knowing that my contract required a year's notice before terminating, I'd written a letter to Larry to this effect. I recall writing the letter several times, ultimately making it short and perhaps too abrupt. This was disastrous; Larry interpreted it as my quitting under fire, whereas I thought my job was successfully accomplished so that I could step out.

As things worked out I stayed at Bell for two more years, getting the bugs out of production and, later, getting Model 42 past its problems. But the main difficulty was with people. It was hard for the company hierarchy to learn new tricks and three Vice Presidents were successively fired before Bart Kelley was eventually put in charge of engineering.

Throughout, the Gardenville group remained dedicated and continued to keep in touch, even when we had to work underground because individuals in management tried to break up the group. It was the loyalty and dedication of the Gardenville group and their successors, not the helicopter itself, that I think of as the main accomplishment, for it is not making a helicopter that counts, it is the process by which it is made, and this resides in people.

Notes:
1945–1947

October 11, 1945

Seen from my flat-car self the panorama of life unfolds with increasing excitement. It is so highly injected with tensions that there is no time to lapse into discouragement. The mouse is eating the mountain.

The monstrous Bell plant is a deserted warehouse—distributed at intervals over its 600-foot length small concentrations of activity show the evidence of Model 47 which is about to be a product.

The excitement of directing many people, the success of the flight of little Ship 3, and now the 42, which paces the air with the dignity and solidity of a Queen Mary—confusion—hyperstimulation, playing two dozen chess games at once, the pawns the remaining 600 workers in Bell, with each of whom I am in intimate touch because I know just what they're doing—which is drilling a particular sized hole in a particular sized piece, amplifying, multiplying the weak input I know by heart—all this—and the personalities of my immediate Gardenville group, men I admire and respect but each of whom has personal idiosyncrasies that hold him chained—all this contrasts with a hunger to be again a-floundering (I was about to say a failure, but I mean unknown quantity). But there is satisfaction in making something exactly the way I want it.

And yet the vista of emptiness which faced me when I turned away from the helicopter—when I looked at my old books at Drifton and tried to pick up the threads of that earlier period—the emptiness and with it the melancholy, bitter turning away from life . . . I was, not afraid, but worried—not that I mind this emptiness, I want it and am willing to pay any price, because I think it is a higher use of the privilege of being alive—worried because maybe to do an about-face with destiny, to take on the monk's robe now, I embrace ineffectuality. For the thought that stabbed most deeply said—thoughts must produce *things,* and what *thing* is there there? Who wants a theory of art? Of what use is it? And now I know a deeper meaning to the use of the word use—it *is* perfectly just to condemn for lack of utility. For what "use" means here is mass in the mental sense. That which is without application, without effect, without utility, without embodiment, is without existence.

That new mathematic that my Faustus yearning seeks.

> With all this I wish for something
> And I know I wish, I'd like to reach
> Up into some unknown upper air, mix
> Numbers there, and obtain flashes from
> Chemicals, clashes from unheard symbols but
> Jimjams and symbols,
> Mixtures and hymnals,
> Squeeze out my mind.

What would it do? The esoteric sword is in my belt, and I use it every day. I reach up and pull rabbits from thin air daily for an audience of trained seals, who stand amazed. Now I want only to amaze myself; I want to retire and seek the esoteric for its own sake.

October 28, 1945

The luxury of being alone in a big house, of moving from room to room "like different planets each has its moon"—of standing here on the edge of time and looking far and deep—toward the abyss that man erects bridges to cross and forever after walks across with no concern, until the elements weaken it again and it has to be repaired—of standing still in the middle of the room, hearing a distant church bell, autumn sunlight on the

floor—of a flashing cacophony of theories coming downstairs
with me like a host of eager dogs—theories that ebb and flow
through me and like blood make me stand erect with their
internal pressure. This luxury, this abyss, these theories, are with
me now.

January 3, 1946

I lay on the couch and felt my body relax. This was the same
body, I reflected, that swam so smoothly on summer nights in
that pond near Princeton when I was eighteen, that suddenly
discovered the fascination of ironing at approximately the age of
five.

Oh, if one could only write. Surely writing is the highest
expression.

But the more difficult thoughts vanish when you try to set
them down—like schoolroom games when the teacher returns.
To write, why? Not to achieve ends, not to create arts, simply to
dig in the dark earth of mind and uncover those succulent
potatoes of meaning.

Reality is crisscrossed with meaning. We see the parade of
events in a pattern of meaning that is inherited from the age we
live in. If in the nineteenth century men dressed in black, it was
because of the discovery of coal. If they wore top hats, it was in
emulation of the locomotive. The discovery of steam, and the
theory of heat that it engendered, dominated philosophy for
years.

And now, only a few months after the atom bomb, I begin to
see that instances of chain reactions are bound to occur. Put
enough uranium together and you have an atomic explosion.
Put enough people on a continent and provide rapid enough
transportation and facilities of communication, and prosperity or
depression spread with explosive violence.

The myth is mightier than the man.

What is unique about me? Like a point in space that has no dimension, only position. Yet I never consider this. Always I am churning, my conscience like a housewife makes butter by churning my innards. Yet what is this churning? It is nothing. I am still a point for all my churning.

Like a river . . . these resolutions and prejudices and laws are stones. Even honor is a large boulder in the river bed, with the current churning around it, eventually dislodging it or else turning in another direction and leaving the boulder as a part of the shore or even in the middle of a field with the river far away. And these fancied laws are really standing waves in the moving current. We see the waves. More closely examined they are full of motion. Life is a moving river. This river is the will of man. It plucks up stones and sweeps them down its churning way.

Look here at this wide valley. You can say if you like that it is life. All we know rests in this flat plane, but do not go away without noting the river over there. This river made this whole valley. It was not always where it is now. But come again, a year from now, and you will see how it has moved.

[During the next three months there was a great deal to do and no time for notes. At Gardenville if a part didn't quite fit, it was modified on the spot. Now it had to be returned to the factory and everybody notified with an ECO (Engineering Change Order), the drawings changed or inspection procedures tightened up, so that assembly of a helicopter was like a king's bed chamber. Then there was the 100-hour endurance test. One helicopter, tied down, had to be run at full power for 100 hours without any failures. If a part did fail, it had to be redesigned and the test begun anew. Another helicopter was assigned a "static test," which consisted of loading each part to several times the load it would have in operation. Then there were tests of engine cooling, vibration, lubrication, etc., and most important of all, flight tests—one machine flown continuously with periodic inspection.

On top of all this, Larry Bell wanted our machine to be the first to have a commercial license. This meant another set of trials under CAA supervision. This we managed to pass, and on March 7 we were given our CAA commercial license—the first to be given to a helicopter.]

March 18, 1946
(Washington, D.C.)

The helicopter having suddenly broken into an unquestioned and acknowledged success with the granting of the CAA certificate—I myself find it fairly satisfactory—and there being no way at this moment that I can occupy myself with it, feeling as I do like a bridegroom at a wedding or a father in a maternity ward, being besides sick with the chemistry of change of state or of shedding a shell or of spring or of love, craving intensely a period of solitude—I would like to go to jail for an indefinite period—I have come here where I propose to adjust my trampled self and prepare for another.

I come to Washington to write in order to organize my activity. As I confront the problem of what to do (recall, please, that we are at a most critical point in civilization), something is needed badly (it is not helicopters). How can I find what it is?

My first thought is that the first step is to postpone all organization. But it still follows that organization is necessary. Even as it was necessary to plan my stay here, to get transportation, a room, money, arrangements to carry on at the plant—so perhaps one must avoid delusions and distractions. If I could depend on the intensity of melancholy depression for purifying, but depression has lifted like a morning fog since I embraced my solitude. This passionate exercise has so changed my chemistry that I'm on a drunken spree and I fear the hangover.

This applies to what has already been turned out. Some thoughts on envelopes written while sitting in the Statler lobby last week, while hopped up with meditation. They now seem thin. Not dead, but padded. Fewer words would have sufficed. It seems too early perhaps to analyze, but time is very short. My trip ends in four days. The world may end in that many years:

In vain I have declared a truce on orange
   juice
and would feign
get some new feet, and try out
a different brain—
   But these, and all my parts
   stay with me still
   and I begin to think the whole
      wide world is
   one continuous paper mill
   rolling a roll of pulp which people
      call the past
   and I will always be harassed.

The idea that the future and the present exist simultaneously as a great factory, where everything already exists, and is established and reacts to other things in a fixed pattern, producing as a result a product, which we call generally the past, is provocative, but it lacks art.

But art is not what we want. Art is value, finish, completeness, where what I want now is force, hunger, inspiration, faith. Art is an enclosure for matter or energy. As such it is complete and bounded like an egg. Its creation is the ultimate goal of human activity, but it is too near in its results—too shortsighted to seize on now. As the end product, it should not be attained until the end, else the result is too trivial.

I am more concerned with my own tropisms at this stage and wish to flounder in new fields. Art will come and must inevitably, as does skill and death. Picasso has said, "I do not seek, I find," and by this he places himself with the great, but also with the dead. For Bing Crosby, like most public figures, is dead, frozen in the solid amber of public opinion—in the state of suspended animation. Therefore I plead—for the postponement of art and for the more serious discontent which now is not, but in due time will also be art.

March 21, 1946
(Washington, D.C.)

Another day of ecstasy. This time all day at the Library of
Congress.

    —Already there is too much to do, and too little time.

    —Concentrate on symbolism.

    —When something is found, photostat it.

    —No time for satire (referring to poems written on envelopes).

    —Internal and External Harmony:
      There is that which has the structure due
      its function, like an automobile or a
      piano, whose form reflects a harmony of
      relations for itself, therefore external
      to man. And that which touches the deep
      chords of human physiology—the beauty
      of the latest clothes, the poignancy of
      a face, the subtle hidden secrecies of
      Hermetic philosophy.

    —Art is boldness, skill, and discretion:
      Boldness of conception,
      Skill of execution,
      Discretion of means (do not ruffle the
      subconscious).

    —But this is not the time for art. We wish to expand. Art is
contraction.

    —Picasso "I do not seek, I find." But what *I* find I throw
away.

March 31, 1946

The great problem is time—I left Washington with high hopes. I could derive unlimited fuel and aid from the ancient mysteries in my plan for the new science. No small part of this was the practice of Oriental philosophy itself. It appeared to be very well expounded in [Manly] Hall's *Self-Unfoldment.*

The first day, Tuesday, I came home unscathed. I had preserved my mental composure and physical energy. In the evening I ordered books. . . . The next day, Wednesday, I started getting enmeshed. I came home about neutral, not tired, but not full of energy either—I had that evening to deliver a talk on the convertible [helicopter convertible to airplane]. The third day, Thursday, I was exhausted—back at the low level I've been for past months. Though I stopped in on Martha [Visser't Hooft], to whom I enthused about my findings—and she retaliated by lending me five new books, which again pose the problem of time—I arrive home to find several visitors who are helicopter customers. It was on this day that Floyd and Dave Forman [Dave Forman, executive at Bell, was assigned the helicopter project. I later met his mother] flew to Toronto— landing the helicopter on the Rainbow Bridge.

I found during the day my old sensitivity coming back and in addition the many-headed dragon of the helicopter seemed to be growing more heads all the time. That evening we went out to dinner and this fruitless waste took my little spare energy. My discourse was on the *true* religion and how Catholicism had appropriated the benefits of symbolism and the magic of miracles, etc., leaving Protestantism barren. To the contention of Stewart that Protestantism had been an error, I held that it was the puberty, the puppy love, of consciousness. Naturally this contention was wasted. The next day, Friday, found me well below sea level, while I kept my chin up for a few hours, revved up Ship 1 with the high solidity blades and took check flights on another model to test the new motor mount. By noon I was in the dumps again. I took a walk through the factory which did not cheer me, although everyone was working on my brainchild. It was as though a dream had become materialized into real people and things and I wandered into it but it still seemed less real to me than the dream I'm now dreaming.

While I've been writing this I've been making plans how to meet this problem of time, for besides the points mentioned there is a rather critical situation at Bell. Management is despairing of getting Model 42 to work in time to design and build the Model 48 [a more powerful version of Model 42] and wants me to undertake it.

I do not entirely trust myself. I recognize that making the helicopter is a cooperative endeavor and I have already erred in underestimating several things which the cooperative action has accomplished. For example, the CAA license which I did not think we could do as quickly as we did. Tom says we paid heavily for it. To function as a member of the team requires not only suppression of most of the satisfactions which would ordinarily accrue to its creator (such as deciding what color to paint it), but a definite limitation to the invention itself: can't invent a better control system because the pilots want conventional rudders; can't make special tests because of tight schedules; necessity for having machine for visitors; necessity not to cross the departmental lines (if one would try to make a flight test, the flight test group feel their prerogatives are being usurped), and many others. All of this makes the work a painful ordeal (another problem is the lowering of morale in my own group, who see departments expanding all around them while I keep my group small).

And there still remains the most difficult barrier of all, the fact that I wish to terminate my helicopter activities by the end of this year or when we get going selling some machines, whichever is first. This wish to have done with it stems from a resolve I made before entering the helicopter field, that I would stay in it only long enough to make it work.

However, my trip to Washington posed the possibility of a solution along the lines of moderation; i.e., to recognize responsibilities toward the helicopter but do other things as well. This is where we encounter the question of time, which leads to certain plans:

1. To economize and cut out all unnecessary waste of spending time.

2. To employ time to utmost advantage.

3. To use all possible assists and helps. That is, if painting, to paint the ideas involved, to use one thing as a ladder to the other.

4. Make notes of everything. The notes proved of great help in the helicopter problem. They served as a container and a focusing device. By this means, too, I can be freed from problems of the day for the study of the mind, etc.

[On April 5th we had our first serious setback. During the routine flight testing of Model 47 (Ship 1), the hub broke—the machine dropped. One pilot suffered a severe back injury, the other was OK. While unfortunate, the wreck gave us valuable information about actual stresses in flight, which in turn made it possible to design the hub for "infinite life."]

April 8, 1946

No progress except a wreck with the helicopter—"listen to the law"—seems to work—can find the law by listening and looking —if I can only keep down the noise of my own thinking—an effort though. . . .

April 10, 1946

The pertinent questions are:

Is work in the right direction necessarily painful, unpleasant, etc.? Granted that work in the sense of effort is necessary (I am comparing what I'm now doing and what I would like to be doing), such as painting, writing metaphysics (or helicopter experiment à la Gardenville). These are hard in the sense that you are driving the lazier part to do the will of the more ambitious part. But I do not call this painful.

But in working with people, particularly a lot of people, I am finding that almost constant suppression of my feelings, exercise of tact, withholding of irritation at stupidities, are necessary. If it were held that this is not necessary and a more positive attitude should be maintained, my impression is that you would not get the same cooperation. One solution is to run things like a military operation and I feel that this must be done in effect, but not openly. The growth of the crop depends on suppression of the growth of the irrelevant ideas. On the other hand, while there is an a priori truth in the "Any plan is better than no plan," which holds with unshakable firmness, there is an unfolding of nature in the pursuit of a new object (flight with helicopters) which must disclose itself to the leader through his people. They are not only his hands, but his eyes and ears through which he senses danger. For example, a man in charge of assembling hubs may be too exacting. Minor slips and carelessness of the production department do not escape him and he just will not slap things together. If it were possible to get him to slap things together and at the same time note what this incurred, it would be ideal. But such men don't exist; they are either careful or careless. He is the eye which signals everything, important or not, to the brain, to be acted upon how it will. If he were not allowed to exercise his prerogative of being fussy, we would cut off our sensitivity (like driving a car while drunk, everything would be easier).

This unfolding means that the concept of the objective (flight in the helicopter) changes and grows. It does not happen by internal growth, *i.e.,* looking in, but by listening to the small whisper of nature which tells those who will listen what reorientation to make. For a given concept to improve or grow it is necessary to adopt a humble attitude, one of readiness to change one's ideas. This is in contradiction to the "military" idea.

This contradiction is difficult enough to deal with, but there is another, the influence of management, which does not see the picture from the same angle. This is to be expected and is as it should be. But it brings about a difficult situation. To progress there must be an undifferentiated protoplasmic tendril which is perpetually reaching up (or down), and this tendril needs the same nourishment as the specialized and useful functions. But because it is unscheduled and has not established a retinue of personnel, it gets no voice in the apportionment of priorities, etc. It is thus continually necessary to be selling management on the need for some new experiment or the need for diverting energies in a new direction.

April 12, 1946

Today things took a bad turn in the morning but I held up and seemed to get through with a new kind of energy. Something has opened up inside me. I seem to be able to float. I get terribly wrought up and feel just as uncontrolled as before; I speak sharply to people, but I'm not depressed. This is possibly the usual fluctuation, but I feel it's a new state. Perhaps I've convinced myself of the nonpersonal attitude. I knew of it, but my vain self had not grasped the idea—until now. Listen.

These notes were intended for nonhelicopter activities—but it is obvious that the self is one piece. My painting has no real merit, does not have my full thought power. The helicopter still is my problem. I must solve it before I reach for a higher type of problem. I am no longer concerned about being able to drop it if I wish. In Washington for five days I never gave it a thought. The problem of the helicopter is now a problem of people, how to exist among them, how to impart the philosophy of mothering this wild son, how to make them listen. For the thing speaks, and then it shouts, but there is a long time between. The observer on the top mast sees, the others must believe. As Martha says, the inner sanctum sees the mysteries the outer church bases on faith.

April 14, 1946

The problem of the helicopter is not finished. It must be made foolproof. But this is not hard.

It resolves into seeing what happens when it is put into the hands of others.

For instance, if the rotor is removed with a crane, there is no stop for the blade and it can be twisted too much and cause bending in the equalizer tie rods [a lever to insure that the hub is centered].

The bar can be improperly assembled.

And so on.

The next problem is people. The soil in which the helicopter was planted was unplowed. The old cornstalks still stand. The new seeds grow, but slowly, because the ground is hard and full of old roots. Gradually the philosophy spreads and one by one we obtain converts. Those branches that are unnecessary or premature get no nourishment from the center and finally drop off. (Service Department, Publicity Department—the rigmarole of synthetic jobs that sprang up when we moved into the Big Plant and jobs had to be created. A factor that is not to be ignored is that people who don't feel they are contributing tend in the long run to quit.)

The third problem is myself—how to conquer sensitivity, how delegate and trust others. As I see it, how to listen to the law, how to insist, how to persuade, how to sell what I hear. How to vanish.

This problem is as near as one can get to higher consciousness. So perhaps the practice of higher consciousness is here at home —the medium is of no importance.

I am beginning to construe this book as a notebook on the machine that is much more complicated and subtle than the helicopter. The machine is my mind and body, with which I experiment every day, through which I will eventually achieve the end I seek, for I always knew it was not the helicopter. Here is a great experiment indeed.

The machine which this book is about must be made to fly.

There is no need for staying in more than an advisory capacity, if the helicopter is a success.

If the helicopter is not a success, it will be because the time is premature or because we overplayed our hand, but it will probably mean financial collapse.

The use of the airplane facilities is a mixed blessing. At one moment Larry is talking about what he owes the old employees. Again what the stockholders want. The interests of the stockholders or the old employees are best served by making the helicopter, as a manufactured product, a success. Only thus can either be helped. Therefore, it is futile to talk about having to accept certain conditions detrimental to the helicopter because we couldn't go back on the old employees.

April 21, 1946

Do you ever suffer a sea pang? A longing for deep water—for
the cool envelopment—the languorous support—the green
translucency? Does the earth seem hard and dry, the sun too
bright? I used to love to swim under water and I even felt
certain types of living were like underwater life—where I was
supported by the medium without effort, not exerting constant
muscular effort to stand up. I feel that life is a trip across a
lighted room, full of laughing people. I awake and must cross in
my nightclothes from one door to another. Or I am a fish that is
trying to crawl across an island to the other side. I will crawl
back into the refulgent deep. The long night of the soul will
come again.

What of this occult learning? It tickles the palate—a sort of
relaxation from the dryness of science. It refreshes and feeds
the organic brain and one judges it to be good. But then what
have we? Certainly nothing positive—no cure for diphtheria; no
formula for making chemicals; no table of elements; no
information on densities, strength, conductivity, hardness; no
drugs, foods, utensils, vehicles; no, nor even a vocabulary—only
a sense of secret drama but all in an unintelligible tongue.

Such are the misgivings, such the outcry of the petty side of
tailored man. How long have we given it? How many rules
copied down, how much trouble taken to learn to touch and
handle these new values—scarcely any. It should have at least
the application and study I gave to helicopters—ten—fifteen years.

To revert again to Bell. Carl [a Buffalo friend, not at Bell]
posed a totally different solution. He cut the Gordian knot. He
was probing me. I said, "Do you know what I feel?" He said,

"No, what do you feel?" I said, "To hell with it, let them jump in the lake—I'm fed up—I don't care if they drop the whole business, I'm sick of it."

This, he said, was good; just say the same to Larry—say you don't want to sign any agreements.

The reason I hesitate to do this is that I fear the answer will be, "What do you want—we'll do it." Why should I dread that answer? Because they don't mean it. What would happen? I would get grudging submission on certain points, yet it's the whole philosophy that's wrong. You no sooner close the front door on something than it's running out the back.

Slowly, painfully, time proves me right. It's not me that's right. It's that I first hear the decision of nature and form my opinion on what I hear. They are listening to other voices that shout much louder—false voices that pull them up blind alleys.

Take the body. Management wants a helicopter to look like a Buick. I am influenced by what is forced upon us by nature. Ship 3 had no body. It worked. Gradually it evolved enough of a body to provide what was necessary—protection for the pilots. The new shape was not only easier to make, gave better visibility, was lighter, but it also had stable flight characteristics. The cabin has been found not to be stable, one more disadvantage.

This is not a matter of a personal battle with Bell. It is more one of unfolding a complex pattern of life to a large group of people—of wooing them against their will to something buried and vaster than they dream. My role, I construe, is to lay open the situation so that they may see with their own eyes.

April 25, 1946

I *cannot* not-work, or assume indifference. It is my nature to want to work hard on a thing, to improve it, to make it approach the divine prototype. But to be hedged about by stone walls, lines of authority, stepping on people's toes, to be prevented from creating, is the deepest kind of poison. This poison is going through me daily.

April 27, 1946

Bell situation is clearing. The role of ghost appeals to me and makes everything come out right. If I am not on a competitive basis with the elements with which I have to struggle, my difficulties seem to vanish. So enough of all that. . . . Somehow I have sidestepped a rolling boulder. It has passed me and now rumbles down the mountainside.

The change came during our conference when it was clear that my difficulties were lost to management. They could form no idea of what they are. Since this is the case, they are either imaginary, or they are so invisible that I will never get someone else to see them—and the struggle vanishes. Because it takes two to make a fight.

This obscure reasoning is just what I'm interested in objectively as well as subjectively.

Fable: Mr. Jones's wife declared she saw a Bojum on the table in their living room. She talked so much about it that Jones began to see it himself and to take an interest in the little animal. He even went so far as to ask its advice on business matters. Sometimes he displayed it to his friends and to his guests at parties. However, most of his friends couldn't see it and denied its existence. But Jones did see it and there ensued a bitter struggle between Jones's friends, some of whom saw it and some of whom didn't. Jones's whole existence became entangled in the controversy and he was miserable.

But Mrs. Smith, who also saw a Bojum, was a more cautious woman. When she found her husband could not see the Bojum, rather than precipitate the situation that was causing so much struggle at the Joneses' house, she said no more about it. Being a kind woman, however, she fed the little animal when Smith was away and derived great pleasure from its companionship. Smith never had any trouble. While he did not see the Bojum, he knew that his wife did, and felt a little ashamed of himself, for he learned to respect his wife's advice, which he suspected the Bojum had given her. The judgment of the Bojum was sound and he always acted upon it. As for showing it to his friends, it never occurred to him, since he couldn't see it himself. And though he knew the source of his wife's intelligence, he did not talk about it and seemed to prefer to credit her—all of which led the neighborhood to respect the Smiths and especially to admire Mrs. Smith, a woman, people said, of rare charm and judgment.

With all the esoteric knowledge nothing is really revealed. If something is said it is claimed that the real meaning is hidden but no one undertakes to say what it is. Blavatsky's commentaries are quite finite. Any intelligent nineteenth-century writer with imagination (this already makes her at least an Emerson or a Huxley) could have done as much. So much for her comments. The verses of the *Book of Dyzan* are high-grade stuff but whoever wrote them does not say much. Is it the process of fertilization or the spiral nebulae? Whatever it is, it is vague generalization cast into symbolism. By comparison actual science is much better, although subject to error. But it seems to me Planck's constant, or the atomic table, or the electron spin, or the energy levels, or the naming of the particles (neutrons, positrons, electrons, alpha particles), or almost any concrete idea of physics transcends the verbiage of esotericism—put in another way, even if false, some physical concepts are more mind-expanding than the occluded occult.

So I am cooling off. A week ago I was a palpitating jellyfish—I'm sorry it's past. I was acutely sensitive, acutely aware—I was panicky, feeling, thinking, but very unhappy. Now the steaming pool has suffered a cold snap, the morning dawns with a thin sheet of ice over its surface. Is this a new winter? Or is it like a warm March and April and a cool month of May? Or has it nothing to do with the season—the crab has grown a new shell?

My new self is a dry bone which I see too seldom and under too great difficulties; never was a creature nourished on such thin broth. If starving out can bring death it will now. Also I detect a slight overstatement for literary effect. Although I crave it—it seems easier to ignore it. Put it this way: a while ago I wanted and needed my new self so I loved it, because of a chemical affinity. But circumstances have starved it out. From platonic it distilled again until it is not even spiritual. I don't know what would happen if I confronted it. If it reached out and touched me, what was warm and organic before would now be thin and hard, perhaps sharp like a razor. How unnatural! How wrong—but what a relief! But I have put on my spectacles. I was never a cynic but I used to say cynical things. Now I feel no urge to say anything but sweet things. Could it be I am a cynic?

What a flop, the higher consciousness; it didn't turn out right. Higher altitude only. A cool view and a greater distance. The air is eager, nimble. The esoteric is my greatest disappointment.

May 12, 1946

A few days ago my new self arrived. It is in some ways a disappointment. It does not seem at all what I ordered. But things are hard to get these days. I dared not return it. My old self was completely worn out. The new one seems hard and crisp like a new pair of shoes, but very comfortable. I suppose after I've worn it awhile it will get like the old self. At this point it seems quite inhuman. Just wait till I've worn it awhile!

The Bell business is still a thorny couch. I suppose a lot of my feelings boil up from the lower instincts—jealousy, filial devotion. It is hard to cut the umbilical cord. My upper brain is not initiating the disturbance. It's the servants' quarters that ring in the fire alarm.

If life can be mortal, why not immortal? The idea of mortality is taken for granted. For the germ, life is immortal. The cell that produces a human being is just as much a being as the man it grows into; it reproduces itself forever, therefore it lives forever. Since it lives forever, it is immortal. It would seem that only growth of the body produces death. Therefore, it remains that to make consciousness immortal one has to go back to the cell. Which is the conclusion of the Buddhists.

Can life have evolved forms that are immortal? Obviously it has. Is not any single-celled animal immortal?

Can life have evolved pure spirits—cells of consciousness that exist forever? Could not these be the souls of men? If there were such forms of life, where would they be? Certainly not here, not walking in the street, not eating food, not treading on the face of the earth. Why not behind the moon? Why not above the clouds—and if there, how boring for them. Would they not out of curiosity come down here and enter into the bodies of people? Yes, perhaps, but why would they stay; why wait for death before they flew away? That's what is hard to understand.

Today I had to get home, I thought, by taking a bus. When I began to wait for the bus, I found there was no money in my pocket. So I walked. My step was light, spring buds burst from my fingertips. The stores along the street slid past me. Coming to my house I said to myself, I live there. Going into the house, I took a drink of water. It was cold. Going upstairs, I lay down for my nap. Sleep came.

Many victories were won today. It happens I feel better. If there is a connection between the two, I am doomed to more sorrow for

If the heart be glad
Because the quest is had,
This is not good. It's bad.

For if that which is alive be placed in a dark hole, surrounded by stone walls, altogether shut off from the light of day and the sweet air, will it not die? Say brother, have you ever seen a potato under the cellar steps?

My Companion: How reassuring it is, how pleasant, after this travail, this long battle, this journey through the wilderness, to have at my side this old friend of my youth, this patient one, who has never spoken, this body of mine. Good friend, how glad I am to see you. Really, it is quite uncanny how long I had forgotten you. Now that I have discovered the new self, I have this friend to introduce. Perhaps you can enjoy each other.

Did not the hunter ask for but a drink from that deep pool? Drinking water should not make him such a fool to want to drown. Let him rise and resume his journey. He can come down again.

Then there is that long narrow passage from the cave, through which he crawls, feeling the narrow confines of the rock, the dripping walls, the terror of constraint—till suddenly the passage ends. There on the mountainside, with burst of light, blinding at first, the eye at last beholds the vista of a valley in the broad sunshine, space unlimited. The mind, long held in narrow places, can scarce comprehend the full cup of plenty, the rich loam of joyous earth, the dark pines which provide a shaded covered way if too much space makes the soul timid or the creature small, the bright flowers and path through grassy slopes—all this at once presented to the cave-bound mind with the sole regret that he, the crawler, now must walk.

The wind that is turning these pages over and over is scarce giving me time to read the contents.

First, there is the besetting doubt of the reality of being and nonbeing. Then there is the dilemma of whether to accept or to reject. Both horns are impossible. Denial, not being true, can't be the solution. Acceptance, being a hollow illusion, is not either. Finally, there comes the solution that it neither is nor is not, that what is there is universal. Its acceptance does not imply its possession. The cave belongs to the cave dweller, but the broad valley is viewed by all. It is so big that those who wander in it will hardly have their paths cross.

May 31, 1946

Yesterday, much as I wanted to do and much as there was to do, I could do nothing, and went to sleep repeatedly while reading Blavatsky. She is not a lucid writer, nor does she say what she wants. There is too much vituperation and obscure reference. I realized I'm coming to need the nervous excitement, the hyperstimulation of the Bell plant. The need for the love of the new self returned when I got back in the struggle again today.

And what a struggle. People fighting over who will take certain blades, who needs the extra hub. The stupidity of the engineers in the elaborate analysis of the control system that was so full of errors. It applied to the old system, happened to be correct for the new, but was never used anyway. The union agitator being watched by the men. The little helicopter which balks at each change made by management.

Slowly, but with gradually increasing tempo, the steps firmly advance. The good triumphs and the wasted bad lies strewn about. Stronger than life, the imponderable myth draws all things to it and like a current pulls the lesser waters to its own. Will its rushing rapids, its precipitous mountain torrent sometime become a quiet stream, a river slowly, majestically, meandering to the sea?

June 2, 1946

Perhaps our own hat is on backward, our own mind too narrow to see.

The situation at Bell is a similar one. The helicopter is growing up all around me, most of the new steps I shriek "no" at happen anyway.

Like an automobile driven recklessly over a bumpy road, I cringe at the sign of each bump, but the car holds up and passes on. Maybe it's hard to push the knife into your flesh. It's not the pain—it's the reflex which disturbs. How hard to lift your own eyelash.

Reverting again to Bell. The fact that I've been right so many times doesn't mean I'm right. The great morsel—the Model 42— has *now* been vomited up as predicted. I should get a photograph of it as it is now, the plush body ripped off—quick repairs bristling like toadstools from a decayed log, and so I triumph, but . . .

June 4, 1946

Cleaning up my desk—from trip to Washington on Statler
envelope:

> Now I feel no pain—and only
> once in a while, tug at the kite string
>   of my soaring brain.
> The teeming street is far beneath me.
> I disdain to let my dangling feet engage
>   the earth,
> that fixed and flat terrain.
> Alack, alas, this mood must be dispelled—
> I have to catch a train.

June 16, 1946

That notion of the temptation of the flesh, which pervades the
philosophy, the ethics of all times, Christian, Buddhist, and even
the esoteric, that notion which refers to indulgence in physical
sensations as something into which the unguarded self slips
easily and to which it goes unless held aloof by the intercession

of higher faculties, is false. At least it seems false to me. I still have a body and I enjoy what it can do but it seems to me that my will is either too timid or too disinterested to take it where it would like to go, for it accurately to be called a case of temptation at all. Modern life I suppose is to blame. My body likes, let us say, to play golf in the country. However the country is some distance away and I have to call for a taxi, or reserve tickets, set aside a suitable time and generally attend to tiresome details so that the temptation of the flesh can be indulged. And then at the last minute when all the plans have been made to take the little brat to the country, I have to call it from something that has distracted it, or laziness or torpor, and slap its hat on and drag it forth. I do not think this is properly a case of temptation of the flesh nor do I think the motherly patience of dragging the child forth is indulgence.

Furthermore, I have a great deal of respect for my body. It brings me dreams of a singular richness. The kisses I impart to the beautiful creatures whom I encounter in my sleep, who are women of understanding and who completely lack personality, are the most heavenly bliss. To say that they are evil is ridiculous. I enjoy with my whole being a flight alone in a helicopter. It is not, however, a temptation because I have to screw up my courage and exercise willpower to do it. It is likewise with the flesh generally, particularly if another person is involved. There are certain exceptions such as losing my temper. But even in those cases where I am out of control there is often a suspicion that my will, or whatever the higher faculty is that controls, is pleased with the course events are taking since it is saved the trouble of driving a lazy body to speak forcefully.

I still have not sufficiently stated the case, for the body is such a wonderful thing that I'm inclined to doubt the whole fabric of the notion of higher faculties.

I venture to say the highest expression of mankind is pure sex. And pure sex is rare. Sex is generally tied up with vanity, one party feels possessive toward the other and the moment is a contract for the future, or one party is winning some kind of credit by the transaction, or there is a sense of obligation on the part of one of the parties. Or perhaps one is a nymphomaniac and completely outstrips the other. But when both hungry people just grab the food for its own sake and for the desperate inner need for it, and philosophy, if it must be present, is a few old codgers who play dinner music in the mezzanine, then we are living.

June 18, 1946

Did I say I inherited the 42? I feel that the Bell situation has clarified almost entirely—though they still annoy! [Model 42. The large helicopter designed by the regular engineering department. In flight it developed various problems which could not be solved. It was finally handed over to me to fix. This encouraged me because it was an admission that the "Gardenville" methods could accomplish what the "system" could not.]

Mrs. Forman gave me Tagore poems. [Mrs. Forman was our next-door neighbor on Oakland Place where my wife and I had a garage apartment. One day, as we were sitting in our back yard, our Kerry Blue, Bryan Boru, chased a squirrel up onto the wall surrounding the yard. To satisfy the dog I put him on top of the wall. He promptly fell over on the other side. I went after him.

As I dropped down on the other side an old lady gave a startled cry, "First the dog drops out of the sky and then you!" It was Mrs. Forman. We became good friends. It developed that Mrs. Forman had spent a year in a Zen monastery, was one of Larry Bell's original backers, and was a friend of Sikorsky.]

> You have set me among those who are defeated
> I know it is not for me to win, nor to
>   leave the game

I shall plunge into the pool although but
     to sink to the bottom
I shall play the game of my undoing.

I shall stake all I have where I lose my
     last penny, I shall stake myself, and then
     I think I shall have won through my utter
     defeat.

Free me as free are the birds of the wilds,
     the wanderers of unseen paths.
Free me as free are the deluge of rain, and the
storm that shakes its locks and rushes
     on to its unknown end.
Free me as free is the forest fire, as is the
thunder that laughs aloud and hurls
     defiance to the darkness.

I sit at my window this morning where the
     world like a passerby stops for a moment—nods
to me and goes.*

The big house is very dark and still. No sound except the dog
scratching—no light—no people—save myself and the maid.
Suddenly the clock strikes eleven—which is misleading because
it is eight o'clock by the hands. Actually the hands are incorrect
too since the correct time is probably about ten thirty. That this
guess is correct is confirmed a few minutes later by the sudden
discharge, like a score of old-fashioned muskets, of the
thermostat, which is the only timekeeper that the furnace and
the hired man take seriously. I feel somewhat hilarious, having
just come from a curious session with the telephone, whose
unvaryingly serious admonition gives little hint of its content
which varies to an extraordinary degree.

     The Chinese philosopher Qung Sin made a pilgrimage to
the greater teacher of Zen, Chawang Tso. Journeying long
he arrived at the gate and was refused entrance. So great
was his zeal, however, that he remained immovable for
seven months, facing the wall. Finally he again knocked on

*Rabindranath Tagore. COLLECTED POEMS AND PLAYS.

the gate. This time the master asked him what he wanted. I desire to know, O sage, what is the nature of Zen? The master was about to hit him with the stick he kept for such occasions when the telephone rang. Chawang Tso was enlightened.

I may say I feel very odd. One side of my face feels very different from the other. My right side seems definitely hilarious, the other sullen. Also my right eye feels higher than my left. (On checking in the mirror the opposite is the case.)

June 27, 1946

My dreaming, thinking, concentrating, worrying—no distinct line between them. Only now the problem is different; I ask for strength, for humility, for patience, for courage, for application to accomplish what is to be accomplished. It is difficult, it is worth any price to succeed in this endeavor (the psychopter). I must abandon everything that could burden and weigh down the leaps that must be made.

What then are the paraphernalia I must lay down? When I was eight years old I collected pencils. I was given a bicycle but try as I would I could not learn to ride. At last I took myself in hand. I removed all the pencils there were, eighteen if I remember correctly, from my pockets. I mounted the bicycle. Success!

This journal is before me because I found it worked before and I am sure it will work again, but I have not been regular, consistent enough in its use. Things flow by so fast, but they must be recorded at all costs. Even if they be very poorly noted they must be noted and dated, for the progress of ideas is more important than the ideas. There are also reasons for using a cipher—but I have not wit enough to invent one I would have patience enough to use.

June 27, 1946

Ideas: The idea of the universality and importance of the analogy remains strong. Let us assert then the analogy as a fundamental axiom of our credo.

Later we can go more fully into the very profound reasons that the analogy is basic; sufficient to note here that it is.

1. The image creates the physiological (emotional) content of the idea. Is there any other content? I doubt it.

2. All things are projections of the self. The image, the analogy, creates new matter by sculpting it out of the material of the self.

3. Even when science clearly and objectively sets down its laws—when it says the atoms belong in the atomic table of elements and have numbers associated, *i.e.,* Hydrogen 1, Helium 2, etc.—by the very act it colors the data and uses the image. (Otherwise why does Russell say one is the class of all classes having one member?)

June 29, 1946

When again a man is about to suffer an injury, if he will
utter the name of Kwanzeon Bosatsu, the sword or the stick
that is held will be at once broken to pieces and the man be
released.

KWANNON SUTRA

Or if in drifting in a vast ocean a man is about to be
swallowed up by the Nagas, fishes or evil beings, let his
thought dwell upon the power of Kwannon, and the waves
will not drown him.

KWANNON SUTRA

All kinds of beings, such as the egg-born, the womb-born,
the moisture-born, those born without form, those with
consciousness, those without consciousness, those with
no-consciousness, they are all led by me to enter Nirvana
that leaves nothing behind and to attain final emancipation.
Though thus beings immeasurable, innumerable, and
unlimited are emancipated, there are in reality no beings
that are ever emancipated. Why, Subhuti? If a Bodhisattva
retains the thought of an ego, a person, a being, or a soul,
he is no more a Bodhisattva.

Again, Subhuti, when a Bodhisattva practices charity he
should not be cherishing any idea, that is to say, he is not
to cherish the idea of a form when practicing charity, nor
is he to cherish the idea of a sound, an odor, a touch, or a
quality. Subhuti, a Bodhisattva should thus practice charity
without cherishing any idea of form. . . . Subhuti, what do
you think? Can you have the conception of space
extending (only) eastward? . . .

If there be a man who, listening to this Sutra, is neither
frightened nor disturbed, you should know him as a
wonderful person.

DIAMOND SUTRA

Well I listened and was not frightened and in fact agreed most
wholeheartedly, since it is very much in accord with the theory
of process, *i.e.,* the perpetual present, and I thought of watching
a spring welling up in a lake with its perpetual throwing out of
form, yet its center being no form or the active principle. Yet
today I was most unenlightened and was torn by my sensitive
pride in dealings with people at Bell—I think I am cured but yet
I notice little stabs of vanity pricking me often. For example, Y.
said he had used the chromic acid dip process in 1936; I replied
I had dipped helicopter parts in 1932 (it wasn't that early, but I
thought at the moment it was), but here was an instance of my
vanity coming out. I felt it was a false note as soon as I said it,
but that kind of thing still occurs. So I'm not free after all—but
the point I'm making is that one can recognize the truth and still
not conquer the chemistry of one's reactions.

But the next Sutra also was good, though perhaps not so
bluntly new (the above ideas are not put forth in the Zen
teachings).

Further, Mahamati, according to the teaching of the
Tathagatas of the past, present, and future, all things are
unborn. Why? Because they have no reality, being
manifestations of Mind itself; and, Mahamati, as they are
not born of being and nonbeing, they are unborn.

LANKAVATARA SUTRA

As I drove out to the plant I asked myself, "Is the helicopter
unborn? Has it no reality? This acorn of the barn in Paoli, is it
not now blowing the morning dew from cherries (it saved the
$6,000 cherry crop), is it not finding ore in Canada? Did it not
inspect as many miles of power line in forty minutes as required
two men two days to inspect on foot? Is this unborn—unreal?"

I suppose I could answer this puzzle if I tried. The point is
that the helicopter is not a form, therefore it is not unreal. If it
be conceived as a form, it slips away, it is unreal. The engineers

always make the mistake of imitating the form, then they are puzzled when it still doesn't work. The thing that makes it work is what is poured into the form—he who steals the form may lose the contents, which are like smoke in a glass. If the glass be moved, the smoke will escape.

June 30, 1946

In the above it is not vanity that is condemned but just the literal interpretation of form. For continually the Sutras refer to the accumulation of merit, to the way to advance oneself. This is refreshing and very sound. For when the Sutra says:

> When a Bodhisattva practices charity he should not be cherishing any idea . . .

that is any idea of form, etc., which would be a technical error. And they say:

> if there were another who listened to this Sutra with a believing heart, the merit of the latter would far exceed that of the former—

So one might practice charity to achieve merit, which would be cherishing the idea of merit. The idea of merit must not be an idea of form.

This is more sophisticated than Christian teaching which would have us deny vanity, and leads to concealment of vanity or its disguise in other shapes. This is impressive.

In fact, these Sutras seem more comprehensible and more profound than the Zen, which in turn is better than the interpretations of Zen made by modern teachers.

July 4, 1946

Mr. [Paul] Brunton's Yoga technique, to concentrate on the state of mind to which we can gain access just as sleep commences, is close to what I've been doing for some time. I find the dawn very stimulating and my mind works very well from about five to seven in the morning, although I'm dozing all the while. Ideas come in fast and I can almost retain consciousness when I go to sleep and the waking ideas suddenly become dramatized and turn into typewriters and automatic relays. Much more concentrated effort will be required before I can get the full benefit, however, and I owe Mr. Brunton the credit for pointing out the special significance of this aspect of living.

I had another dream which while not prophetic was rather pretty. D. and P. were talking in the parlor. I noticed a large bat on the wall near the floor with its wings spread. "Do not be alarmed," I said. "I will remove the bat." So going over to the wall I grasped it firmly in both hands and carried it into the kitchen. The kitchen had two doors and I asked F. to open the door facing the strong wind that was blowing, because I realized the bat would have trouble taking off downwind. Waiting for F. to open the door, I found I was losing my grip of the bat which now had become a beautiful bird with iridescent colored feathers like a peacock. Its head still had a ferocious appearance, for it had a heavy curled beak like a vulture. As I held it it struck me with its beak, though not hard.

Besides the dreams I had a new set of ideas this morning. It seemed to me I was getting complicated inside. I could feel the world welling up inside of me, pushing myself into the background. It was host to a lot of new things which were demanding attention. I was so busy seeing to their needs that myself was being pushed back. . . .

This was another beautiful morning, like the one when the day was getting ready for man to come and walk through its garden. Grooming the face of nature so that man could muse on his problem. And it seemed to me also that I must retire into myself, hide from the active world, and concentrate on achieving what won't work, on doubtful theories, on those wonderful things that are not yet settled. Why? Because only in this realm can you move creatively, for in this region the light is dim and no one sees you move, hence the freedom. "Ghosts move at dawn." And back in the exotic jungle, the untrodden world, fantastic forms walk and climb. Monkeys talk; great beautiful birds glide through the trees; orchids crawl around the tree trunks; my antlered soul nibbles rare sprouts and pokes its way through strange familiar shrubbing, not fearing the tiger because he too is just another fantastic animal. Also I am subject to hallucinations more than ever. Under hypnosis, when we are told our hand is in the fire, we feel the burn and even have the skin blister (I've heard). The ideas I get now each day demand a new solution. Yet when the next day comes the illusory nature is apparent—and the more convincing the hallucination the less it is to be trusted.

July 13, 1946

The pressure of gloom and melancholy is removed and with it the push which helps to write and think. But I feel I am making progress. A few days suffice to show *change.* That's not what I mean. I refer rather to a difference which still shows up when change is discounted. Thus from day to day the change due to depression and elation, likes and dislikes, positive and negative, is most apparent, but progress is the different plane of appreciation of the same object contemplated through the same mood.

Evidence of this has been filtering through to me. My handwriting is looser and freer. Paintings and ink sketches more direct and expressive. My attitude toward people more open and unguarded. I dreamed last night I was swimming with a lot of people. I was stark naked and most of the others wore bathing suits. I was perfectly comfortable about the situation. A few dark-skinned Italians were also naked.

The dead cat on the road seems less a tragedy now. Life is universal, interconnected, one expanding puddle; dead things are places where the puddle has stopped, but the body of moving fluid is behind them connected everywhere with itself, pushing, expanding, changing—death is a dead end. So, too, an obsolete part; the limb dies on the trunk, but the trunk remains feeding other fruit through other outlets. Hence the idea of immortality is always associated with the idea of loss of self. For that which dies and that which is immortal are separate and distinct. If we can learn to lose our selves in life, then death is not the end.

July 14, 1946

Now I am comfortable; the crystals of meaning are all held in solution and I have nothing to say. Yet the appetite, the desire, to lay some egg is present as much as ever, and I sit brooding but hatch nothing.

July 24, 1946

Instability of whirling shaft—an image which represents response of the human spirit to stimuli like love, hate, greed. At higher speed the shaft is stable against forces impinging upon it. At lower speed there is partial disturbance. At the critical speed it is unstable.

Let us say that the incident stimulus creates a disturbance, which is slightly more than no reaction, *i.e.,* the nonrotating shaft. This would represent, let us say, affection, puppy love, mild stimulus.

As the shaft speed increases the stimulus causes a greater reaction, which can be infinite (in practice there is always damping and hence not infinite response), and which corresponds to the rate at which the shaft would vibrate (*i.e.,* stimulate itself).

When the speed gets higher, the stimulus causes a negative response which becomes increasingly smaller, tending toward zero.

This would also apply to a vibrating reed excited by a varying frequency. But in our case what comes from outside is a transient or single stimulus, and the variation is in the receptor, in this case a person.

Now what have we? A spectrum of states of the human spirit. (Speed of rotation of the shaft.) A particular state called the critical state must be passed through which is such that the time required for physiological self-oscillation, "reaction time," exactly equals the time for a complete revolution of the spirit. At this critical state or speed the mind is completely responsive. Only the damping of external obligations, "breeding," etc., offers resistance to complete acceptance. Energy may be absorbed at this point. However, if the stimulus goes on to a higher speed, the psychological speed (reaction time) is exceeded, and response is negative.

At Bell a metamorphosis is occurring which matches my own. Since the Model 42 was handed to me and after my modifications caused an immediate improvement in the ailing patient, I am treated with growing respect and deference. It is hard not to be moved by this. My suggestions about persons to head a Rotor and Control group and a Transmission group have been put in effect, which means a complete reorganization. A softening up is in evidence in the Flight group; when I make a flight request, it is enacted with alacrity. As this grows, so I grow to fit it and become more patient, less personally attached to ideas. Gradually the whole surface is becoming covered with this fluid—like milk poured in the bottom of a pan. A certain area or sphere that is not mine which may be likened to a still dry portion of the dish gets surrounded. The milk first moves around its sides, closes in behind it and then contracts upon it. Most of the machine and procedure originally was mine, let us say 60 percent. What remains becomes mine because the area around it is, but "mine" is not mine, it is the "thing" to which I am servant. It is only identified with me because I am first to get mixed up in it. So what I think of has this inevitable way of coming about because I recognize the inevitable before others become aware of it, being in a better position. As I've noted before, discovery is simply being first to see the inevitable. So the opposition, which is based on entrenched notions and tangents thereto, is eventually displaced.

The inventor does a very simple thing. He poses a question to nature, listens to the answer, then writes it down. Those who follow endow him with prophetic talents because asking the question he has asked, they get the answer he has written down. The error is first in not crediting the inventor for having asked the question, which is the real step, and second in crediting as prophecy what the inventor has merely observed.

The effort toward nonidentification, getting out of the competitive plane, has the result of doing the opposite. Anna in

Anna and the King of Siam, having lost her own child, becomes mother of all the court children, mother of the wives too, and the ideas she is the vehicle of hold greater sway than when her child lived.

There! Now we are ready for the next one. Which is that this marriage, being so blessed with children, makes the new love more impossible.

August 16, 1946

Time has passed, carrying a beautiful vacation.

Also a trip to Philadelphia by helicopter, which was interesting, beautiful, exciting, with an Alice in Wonderland feeling of growing very large so that I could step around the world I used to live in with giant steps.

But time in her passage brings the unexpected, the sudden and terrific tragedy of Milt [brother of Floyd] Carlson's instant death. He waved to the farmers and a few seconds later was dead. Here it is. I sit finally in the chair of life. I almost let my whole weight down. After a while the shock of hearing about Milt, which punished my body with strong glandular injections, left me looser. I felt my skeleton walking with its loose skin and muscles, as though throwing myself into a snowdrift I walked into the city. Yes, I said, I am responsible for his death. [The cause of the crash was never determined. We could find no structural failure or malfunction.] But who can hold it against me? And I felt that the world of people would support the one who has received wounds from the battle of man. I felt perhaps that many would live vicariously in the drama of the inventor of devices that kill people, as they live vicariously in the marriages of crowned heads, in the goings on of movie stars.

So I say I almost sat in the chair of life and I felt that if I could sit in this chair, I might reach something very new.

Only a month ago the problem (of the helicopter) was drying up. I was rising above it. Anyway, it was a personal problem— me against nature, which included the rest of mankind, which I was beginning to feel I had vanquished. *Now,* it might be me and mankind against the problem—and the problem is large again. Philosophy could not teach me this. It took the intensification of trouble. One would expect that lifting oneself above the mundane problems of life, out of the level at which problems loom so large as to obscure the horizon, would be the Way. But now I think I have seen why it is not, and the Way is that relaxation of the ego, or annihilation of self-centeredness, which I say is to sit down in the chair.

Years ago I kept denying access to "that hand that knocks, on my private door, saying to come, repent."

August 19, 1946

I'd had a very trying day. I felt that life was pushing its torture to the extreme limits of endurance. I felt more indirect from my senses. Pushing my sack of bones like an old wheelbarrow.

Suddenly I was energized by an idea. Bart had said we ought to get more people working independently on the cause of the wreck. I said, it never happens, that hoped-for new idea from another brain. Then I outlined my theory. Ideas are like cities along a highway. You move from one to the next with inevitable sequence and each person must have the same development, the same history. Various objections were offered. There are forks in the road. No, I said, blind alleys, but not forks. An idea that does not lead to another idea is a blind alley, fruitless. Bart mentioned the stability. I said, I'd done just what Sikorsky had done, only gone a step further.

I challenged Bart for an example of a new idea coming from a source separate from the main stream. The Landgraff helicopter was instanced and I countered with Hiller having adopted the see-saw rotor. At any rate, the significance seems far-reaching. If I can establish that ideas have this character, this inevitableness, they must exist and be ideas of a mind. That is all a mind is, the ideas in it, and since ideas are predictable, the *mind* I'm talking about, the superconsciousness, exists apart from thinkers. Therefore spirit, which is this consciousness, exists. Its world is the spiritual world, etc.

Talked yesterday to Bart about life after death, etc., including reference to multicellular and unicellular consciousness. It appeared most difficult to think of memory as unicellular, principally on account of association, which is obviously not unicellular, although the quasi-memory of, say, blood cells in their ability to develop immunity was an instance of cellular memory. Bart further instanced the energy states of the nucleus as an instance of memory in the atomic realm.

I kept goading him for a mathematical conception which would permit consciousness to exist after the physical components of it are annihilated. We got nowhere. Then I thought of my theory of the imaginary part of real things, which is that the concept of the thing exists after it is destroyed. For example, if the telephone exchange in Madrid is destroyed by bombs, the condition of affairs is not equivalent to the nonexistence of the telephone building in 1500 A.D. For in 1946 the destruction of the telephone building will bring into play powerful forces which will reconstruct it. If it is objected that the telephone building is a part of a telephone system, hence the system is only, as it were, wounded, we can easily find instances where the complete destruction is accomplished. Say the automobile, if this were annihilated utterly, society would be completely upset; in 1500 no one missed it. There is, therefore, a negative or imaginary part of an object, which is the need for this object. This is just as much a part of it as is its "physical," or real part. This aspect also has to be built, *i.e.,* someone had to develop the need for the automobile, the public demand, as well as the mechanical article and its process of manufacture.

[Later this idea became central in my book *The Geometry of*

Meaning: the relation between the concept of an object and the actual object is a right angle. However, I had not at this time distinguished between the concept ($\sqrt{-1}$) and the need (-1).]

This offers a clue to a kind of existence which continues after the destruction of the real part. But it is only a hint. One interpretation would simply say that when Abe Lincoln dies, the memory of the man, his works, his achievements of thought, etc., live after him. That may be all we can extract from the analogy. [Paul] Brunton and the others, however, are talking about something else.

I asked Bart whether he believed in the afterlife. He said he hadn't thought about it. Probably not. I asked him how he made moral judgments—he surprised me by asking when does one make moral judgments. We were by this time having lunch and were joined by Dave and later by others—conversation went into a steep glide—finally landing on terra firma of tennis.

August 24, 1946

Situation at Bell highly charged. Pilots' changes include items which will take considerable time and are justifiable only on grounds of appearance. They wish it applied to all including experimental ships, which means we'll be delayed on the very important flying in advance of the product machines. Everyone agreed on this but the desire to satisfy the pilots takes precedence.

I am in the same situation all the time, for the machine and every detail of its design is open to public comment. Particularly since the product engineering group is on the verge, as it were, of redesigning it, they are continually proposing changes. Many of these are based on a lack of understanding of the problem, so that I have to defend the original design.

August 25, 1946

Talked to M., recently brought in to head engineering. Told him I admired his ability to withhold his opinion, draw people out, and make decisions accordingly. He became more communicative and explained he had learned over a long period to withhold his own ideas and play the game, which he likened to golf, of getting others to see an idea under their own initiative. It was interesting that he spoke of enjoying this game. I have also found it good sense and apparently the proper solution, but fail to derive pleasure or satisfaction from the pursuit. It is a distilled pleasure, perhaps a civilized one, but there is a certain rawness in my own appetites which I intuitively feel is important—a sort of primitiveness that is necessary in order to retain access to more fundamental issues.

As we continued our discussion I found M. himself suffering from the very trouble he talked about, at least when we got to more fundamental issues, which had to do with how to keep O. in the company, how to set up a helicopter aerodynamics group. He voiced his opinions without listening to mine. These opinions were traceable to his fundamental concept of unification of airplane and helicopter functions, which may or may not be sound. The point here is that he was not open to suggestion, or rather to the reasons why his concept may not be the best. So that I'm now inclined to think that the reason he purred when I made the particular compliment I did was that I'd touched a vital point, one in which a struggle existed and for which the issue was still in doubt. Certainly I've found him quite impenetrable on more basic judgments involving psychology, although very perceptive on purely engineering ones.

About the idea of automatic flight to test helicopters: M.

interpreted Bell as thinking the helicopter incomplete without a pilot, that they must be flown with pilots. Which I don't agree is an answer. It is a *machine* for flying. Certain points can be proved without the need of a pilot. You can roast a pig without burning down a house.

The issue may be rather trivial so far as the ultimate goal of the helicopter is concerned. Perhaps a lone fight to make an automatic flight would simply absorb energy—my energy—and be to my own worst interest. Fundamentally I am trying to get out of the helicopter not because it is what it is, but because I believe in the *psychopter.* The construction of the psychopter is not advanced by plunging again into the helicopter. It is advanced by learning to distill the helicopter. So that from the point of view of the psychopter, which is the important one, the only commitments toward the helicopter which should presently be stressed are indirect ones.

I get a satisfying gratification out of writing these notes. They take the sharp edge off despair, they fill one with a sense of well-being like healthy exercise or normal work, which I always used to do. Now the lack of satisfaction through daily work perhaps is related to the penetrating sense of despair and futility. Years ago I realized that exercise was an indulgence, that I must root it out, which I did, and my energies became absorbed in more mental activity. But is this intercourse legitimate? Have we not failed if we have to sweat out higher aspirations? Perhaps we should sit and gnash our teeth, fanning the spirit fire to whiter heat, not draw it off on intellection and words. But there is some value to the words. They are crystallized ideas, ideas precipitated out of solution, which, as they find expression, acquire a form, and as they become a form unburden the active principle.

So it is wrong to take this attitude against work. Work is a necessary form of activity. It is the trucker who takes away the products, the milker, the reaper and binder. The creative principle has to be drained of its products, otherwise it festers. There is no other way, only we hope for a better brew, a higher distillate than we've been getting. The technique for this is not known; the higher distillate may result from more bottling up, but it is more likely that it would result from removing the lower.

August 31, 1946

After two days as above—waking up cheerful, becoming discouraged—I awoke discouraged and became more cheerful as the day wore on. Stan Hiller [a rival helicopter designer] was here on the 28th. His freedom I envied. The next day was gloomy. A party that evening. I felt more keenly than ever utter despair. I was very polite and solicitous to our guests. I conversed with each in turn with no interest in them, but I feigned one and brought them drinks and sympathetic attention (the case of the Merry Wives of Windsor—Buffalonians). My new self was in front of me, beside me, at dinner, drifting among the guests. I could not face it. I could not reach it, have it, so nothing was to be had. Life was death. Desire was wrong because it was illusion. So I would make no effort of the spirit. I would keep out of life, hide behind a bush and watch my bag of bones move about and toss like a pebble in the surf's undertow.

I'd used the same device at the plant. A sort of act of imprisonment upon the will, the self's leader, so the other inhabitants, the underdogs, the rabble, the rival pretenders, could have their day.

Yesterday I began to feel a new kind of pleasure emerging. This abnegation of self—the rigid suppression of the ego, which seeks its desire, its flattery, its gratification in various forms, especially with no creation—had been accomplished, I said to myself. Perhaps at last I'd broken through the veil of illusion. I could feel that now I would want to do things for others, not because I wanted to benefit them but because there was no one else to do things for, since I'd killed myself. Also I felt removed from the world. Dinner seemed terribly confined. I wanted to be alone.

I might also note that Priscilla [my first wife] and her cousin had come to the plant to pick me up. I'd shown them through the factory. The helicopters on the assembly line, the succession of fixtures for building the fuselage, the hundreds of forgings in bins being machined—in every direction a part that had grown out of my own brain, some of them forms that had never before existed. The emotion was overpowering, accented in me to the point of tears because Priscilla, generally apathetic, felt the impact. This is confusing. One would think I'd be happy. But this seems to be the source of the trouble. Because these things are precipitated out of me, I have to die. Their existence is not consistent with my existence as a living thing. They become a foundation on which others walk. If I move, I create a panic. Therefore, I must be still. I dare not move.

This morning all this hallucination is gone again. I am back to normal—even a little put out because my latest illusion has evaporated. The program of self-denial seems too hard to follow. I reach out my hand again, once more to touch the old established illusion. The new self and other familiar aches and pains.

This most recent misery is in large part induced by not being able to apply my solution to the problem of structural soundness. The humiliation of not being given a machine, unquestioned, to do with as I want, has several aspects. It calls for developing a different technique of getting what I want, the technique of not wanting it with my willful self. It is counter to my desire to get away from the helicopter. That is, the more I continue to participate in helicopter activity, the more I'm depended on and the longer before I can pry loose. And, of course, another aspect: I am not adjusted since I endow a situation with human properties. A primitive instinct. My answer so far is to resign myself, just to hold myself back, to guide and assist but not to oppose, to use a jujitsu method. Hence, the self-annihilation. The only way I can then say I'm getting away from the helicopter is that I'm working on the psychopter within the helicopter. I experiment with the self instead of with the machine.

But maybe the self-annihilation must be narrower—the ideas that come from the self are not to be annihilated, only the self. That means renewed efforts to obtain a ship for automatic use.

Jack Woolams, Chief Test Pilot for Bell, has just been killed in a P-39 airplane souped up for the races. Morning paper was my first knowledge. Plane blew up last night at 6:00. I may say I was afraid of this. But I don't feel depressed by it, probably because it is none of my doing. Its significance is that it was a structural failure. The time is ripe to reopen my request for a ship to test without a pilot.

September 2, 1946

Read Jnana Yoga yesterday and now Indian philosophy—Radhakrishnan.

The latter, rather different from the rest of recent books, is more of an academic review of Indian thought. As such it is open to academic summation, interpretation, and criticism. I feel myself becoming again a scholar or the shadow of one as it occurs during college training.

More generally, the body of Indian thought is coming into existence for me. From an amorphous mass certain distinctions, certain specifics, take shape (is the whole thing there before or do the distinctions create it?).

> Development is only the unfolding of what has already potential existence.
>
> RADHAKRISHNAN

I would say no. Development can entail birth of something altogether new.

September 4, 1946

Tonight I saw *Henry Fifth*—a moving picture. I confess that, in Henry's incognito stroll through the camp on the night before the battle, I saw my own walks among the army working now on the helicopter. Today, for example, starting after lunch, I went to witness testing a Model 42 gimbal ring. It was not ready so I strolled through the shop. I talked to the man who has been drilling the holes in the gear spiders all summer. He now had fixtures and a quicker method. After talking, he said, "Are you from tool design?" But I said not. Then I saw one of the shop foremen, and asked about a 42 experimental part. Then the man making bevel gears. They are coming well. Then a machinist making masts. Then one boring them. Then the big Warner Swaseys on one of which hubs were being machined (he told me he's made two hundred already without changing tool bits), then some conversation with the second Warner Swasey operator making blade grips—eight minutes each [and so on; my notes list thirty items and the next day, fifty].

During the day Model 83, the secret jet airplane (25,000 pounds gross weight, cost about $200 per pound), crashed, making a twenty-five-foot hole in the ground. The airport alarm went off, causing everyone to rush out to wait for the crash, which, however, occurred some miles away, despite a waiting line of fire trucks, ambulances, etc., at the airport. The ship crashed on a farm and the explosion blew the farmer off his tractor, and it was said he was still shaking when they interviewed him. The pilot was uninjured.

Prakriti—fundamental substance out of which the world evolves. Is it protoplasm?

There appear to be many schools of Hindu philosophy

differing widely from each other. They suffer from a dearth of actual "ideas"; they seem fruitless. The contributions of positive science loom very large against this wordiness and intellection. However wrong science may be, for pure invention it deserves a high place. This *invention* which rises as far above the statue of man as a skyscraper above a thatched hut, creates a rich lore, a mythology of its own. It creates the microscope and its world, the telescope and astronomy, organic chemistry, etc. This culture in the West, while it outstrips the mind and leaves it a poor relation, does not exclude the growth of mind far beyond its primitive proportions, for it offers an expanded dimension in which to grow. This growth may never occur but it is tempting, indeed obligatory, to think that the mind should now strive to grasp, digest, and make into mental substance this prodigious orphan, monster if you will, it has created.

Viewed broadly, the essential clue to the tremendous growth of Western science, which is not just science, but its application, is the creation of a small gadget. This gadget is the link which ties the work of one individual into that of another. In the East, which has no such gadget, the greatest works were works of individuals, which remained like giant boulders on the plane of time. But here man has somehow learned to build on the building stones laid by his predecessors; he has learned to use the work of others, though admittedly he does not understand and has gained no intrinsic mental power beyond that of the primitive creature who started it all. He has either coordinated the delusion of his forebears, or has unearthed a shape whose reality is attested to by the fact of its continued stability after successive additions of many larger building stones.

For example, the early chemists identified certain elemental constituents or atoms. A next generation found the atoms could be arranged into a regular table of elements; it seemed as though each element had a unit weight which was a multiple of the first of the series, hydrogen, despite the fact that there were exceptions and discrepancies. The next generation found the reason for these discrepancies, set up the table, and showed the absolute correctness of the initial assumption when the whole story was known. Thus was built either a fantasy of momentous proportions, a fantasy to the third power, or man was dealing with reality (though admittedly he never saw what he was dealing with).

The mental gymnastics of Socrates and many redefiners of the nature of reality seem childish alongside of this accomplishment.

And the above is only one street in the city of modern science. There are hundreds like it—electromagnetic waves for example. A kind of entity was invented which not only did much to explain the long-familiar light and heat, and the newly discovered Hertz waves, but a place was made for many more undiscovered kinds of radiation. If this is a dream, it doesn't matter about reality.

Lord knows I am against scientists, and science to some extent; but as fiction, the contributions of science loom very large.

Perhaps I should consider the point already won; there is no need to reiterate it. Then again, that's not the point here. Two brothers set forth in opposite directions to find the secret of life. One was humble and looked where his vanity told him it was not, in the mud, in putrid meat, in diseased animals, in vulgar mechanic arts; the other was proud—looked within his own temple, found little. They come together at last; the first now is rich and proud, the second poor and humbled, but still neither has the secret. Maybe the second should recognize the findings of the first, and the first should not forget that it was his humility that brought him where he is.

Bart remarked on the way home that it had been a quiet day because the increasingly nervous M. had not been in evidence. For me it was a much better day than yesterday, which for some reason was Hell, and put me in the frame of mind for Jakob Boehme. I wanted to write more about the effect of this upon me.

To put it in a word, I have opened the door to that knocking I used to hear. "That hand that knocks on my private door, saying to come, repent." I felt now I must repent, repent for having made this Frankenstein, for having lived in my own rage these many years. Now, too late, I have become aware of the sun, the world of light, in which we acknowledge a greater authority.

Was disturbed at lunch by Bart's news. Pilots have a new

crab. They don't want fuel lines under the fuselage, but I got
over this easily, possibly because I had not liked it myself. It
will cause another pandemonium in production. Also more
discussion of a new mount for Ship 3. As I went through these
duties, I thought how much it is getting to be a matter of
working through others. I was tempted to see Larry on the
basic question of experimental ships, especially the automatic
flight idea, but held back because there were signs of others
being concerned about it. I have by now definitely decided
on the yielding course, probably because of my nature, but
ostensibly because the alternative offends my sense of timing,
opposes my earlier wish to escape the responsibility for what is
not my own folly (if folly it is—I refer to the *modus operandi* of
management), and there is still the hope that all will work out
in a "democratic" way since the task is great and I have erred
many times in underestimating the power of other people.

Reasons are always suspect, especially when there are several,
for rationalism is a thief in the dark, but there is a general
confirmation of the yielding way in these esoteric influences like
Boehme—who speaks of the light which is the light of the sun,
the light of God's will, to receive which we must surrender,
abandon, our own will.

But I also feel I cannot trust Boehme's grim rejection of all
forms of the flesh—or anyone's for that matter. However lofty
the spirit of God in man, it cannot so turn itself against the
aspirations, the hungers, to confine us forevermore to a hermit's
cell, with no life in us but the wan smile of the chastened
ascetic. There must be some treachery in that emasculation
which removes the taste for life and substitutes in its stead
a sort of self-hypnosis, a druglike asphyxiation of the life
processes. I cannot rightly set up this hue and cry about death,
for this has happened to me before—in 1926, in 1928, twice I
turned my back on all that had gone before and faced a grim·
start from the bottom. Life came back in time, but somehow
never with total conviction, that is, life as it is now has not
been totally convincing since these metamorphoses. The life I
felt was Marlowe's "Sweet Analytics thou hast ravished me,"
until Sweet Analytics appeared in person. Now life confronts
me again, and again I turn away. Why can't I make some pact
with it and get in gear?

September 6, 1946

Why is there no direct mode of expression, no outlet for the pestilent appetite? I turn, this way and that, beating on the walls of my confinement, each way shut in by solid bars. I try to fly; my stumpy wings fan a small quantity of air. I try to think; my mind, like a schoolboy coming home, throws stones at lamp posts, kicks the dust, buys chocolate bars or climbs a tree. There is no handhold on the glassy walls that close us in. I can conceive of how it's done, by patient training, by discipline to perform an ordered precise mechanical step, gradually through squeezing the faculties into a mold to obtain the expected shape, but why—oh why—can we not make our anguish cry a call that is its own perfection, its own joy? Why can't we soar by natural fulfillment through the empty air without the poultice of pedantic medics and a ton of wheels and levers.

September 7, 1946

Ask for a miracle and have it come.

[Howard] Brinton, also Boehme, Radhakrishnan, refer to creation of duality as the necessary step to self-consciousness. In the duality there is the horrible rawness of the wound; that which did not exist becomes exposed to the air; the hideous bloody sight when the head is severed from the body, and when the head is restored the hideous sorrow and rawness and strife, the horrible lashing of entrails, vanish and the head and body rejoin in being one. Oh God. We realize, being one again, that that horrible division has passed. Like having just missed a terrible automobile accident, the heart leaps during the ghastly interval when the duality is apparent; then the moment passes, the gaping wound in reality closes, and there is a tremendous flush of happiness and relief.

September 12, 1946

"But something has happened to me lately that has made me believe that I must offer myself again to do the work I'm cut out to do," I said to Dave. He acquiesced and I was surprised how easily the thing fell into my hands. It was a request for a ship to make the automatic ship. Even Floyd, with whom I anticipated a battle, was cooperative. What was this something that had happened? Before I said it, I knew only subconsciously that it was so, that is, the thought had barely formed and I was surprised that it came out in that way. Yet it was very true. The something has to do with my new self which I had tried to get away from and had come to realize was now part of me. It had to do with the realization that I am also the only person in the world and therefore must not hold back.

Also this morning I faced my new self again. It is a miraculous thing. In the midst of its own difficulties, it reaches out and helps other people with total disregard of the effort required. I am shaken with admiration for it. I even suspect it at times of having a condescending attitude toward me, yet it seems to need me, genuinely, which gives me strength.

Another surprising adventure into the bowels of the Bell

plant. Curious about the printing of the manual, I went to find
how it was made. Found the Art Department much enlarged,
making pictures, printing, busy as beavers on the Model 47
Helicopter Manual. So much that hangs from such a slender
thread.

September 15, 1946

Ouspensky says that Yoga needs a teacher, that once taken up it
must be pursued with all our time, all our energy. And there
was one more caution which I do not recall but which also hints
dire consequences with taking up of Yoga.

My defense is twofold. First, I am desperate now. The past
year has been a great ordeal. It has driven me from one false
resting place to another until I am ready to abandon all. I no
longer have anything except a dutiful attitude about the success
of the helicopter. I'd as soon see the whole thing vanish into
thin air and charge it to experience. The real juice, making it
work, which was a keen pleasure, an indulgence perhaps, is all
extracted. What remains is not mine.

Secondly, I am already part way on the Yoga path. I know
this because of the similarity or equivalence of my conclusions.
My greatest ambition until recently, and in a modified form still,
is to find and name the laws of the mind, which are the laws of
reality, and I now find these have already been worked out, not
perhaps in the same way, but in other ways—

September 20, 1946

Yesterday Ship 1A with new rotor a great success. Constitutes a major improvement.

An incident occurred which brings home the limitation of rationalization. I had calculated the amount of blade shift or mass alignment needed and modified the blade and grip to give about 90 percent of what was desired. The actual displacement was 13/16 of an inch. When I flew the ship the improvement was remarkable. There was no question about it. As I came back into the hangar the engineer rushed forward to tell me he'd found a mistake in the calculations. It should have been only 3/8 of an inch. We had moved the blade more than twice what we should have, so it should have been worse instead of better. We went in to the board. A new error was found that increased the desired distance. Then we found we omitted something else which when taken into account indicated the blade should not have been moved at all. We decided to measure the blade center of gravity again and start all over.

Reason is disposable tissue. Use it for colds, etc.

September 21, 1946

Calculation straightened out now with center of gravity measured correctly. The offset in blade root according to calculation is exactly what we made. Further flying of ship with friction removed confirms the pronounced improvement.

October 2, 1946

Read Bible—Matthew—last night and found it very impressive. It seems impossible to accept Christ without his miracles. And the parables are no less impressive. So we reason like this. The parables represent concrete evidence of a creative genius greater than we can measure—exceeding anything before or since. The miracles we have only on say-so—but the fact that the parables are "miraculous" makes the miracles only a physical counterpart or comparison to the miraculous parables. In other words, because of the evidence of the parables we have no choice but to assume that a person of supernatural powers was there; that being so such a person would have been capable of miracles. This is not self-evident, but it is almost so. I am convinced even on the basis of my own small world that a greater understanding of natural law permits the accomplishment of things which to the outsider appear as "miracles." It is relatively unimportant how the doer interprets his power. He may (as in the case of

Houdini, Dunninger, or a mixture of mind reading, etc.) *profess* to be using natural law entirely (it is all law, supernatural law would not deny natural law), or as in the case of saints, etc., profess to accomplish the effects through faith in God, or as in the case of purely scientific accomplishments such as Pasteur, Tesla, etc., to be acting entirely in the "law," which is not a law at the time but a new discovery not accepted by the academic body of science.

I say it is unimportant how the doer *interprets* his power; perhaps I mean it is not for him to interpret. He is the vehicle of the supernatural power, and may even ascribe it to diet, for though he be infinite in his own field he is no more than ordinary when he becomes his own interpreter.

So we have to settle whether we believe in *miracles* or whether we believe in supernatural persons. It seems to me miracles are acts of supernatural persons. To them they are not "miracles"; they know how they are done. So miracle is a relative term. (I hardly need talk about what the savages would think of an airplane, or a steam roller or a walkie-talkie, etc.)

So we must recognize the supernatural aspect of Christ. Modern religion has overstressed the fact he was a "good" man; his goodness was only secondary. He gave himself for man—hundreds would do this. I feel it is wrong emphasis. Rather he worked out a whole plan, one step of which was his crucifixion —perhaps he did not really die at all, but simply acted death.

I see if I keep on like this I will have to throw over my theory of time being outside of all structure. So that even God cannot predict. Christ prophesied that Peter would betray him three times before the cock crowed, but let that go for the present.

Further, I find the Gospel according to Matthew better literature than most Buddhism. This is because it is better reporting—it deals with actual events and quotes, the actual words of Christ. While Buddhism, especially Zen, makes much of the words of various teachers, the setting is murky, the ideas vague; it lacks the essential action and clarity of the New Testament. Does this betoken that greater power of the West toward accomplishment? The Chinese invented gunpowder—but did not use it. Well then, they didn't really invent it. Perhaps the sinful abuse of gunpowder to kill, etc., etc., is unimportant. The West found, investigated, developed gunpowder and hence extracted the special essence of it and are therefore more alive to it. The East discovered it but went no further. Gunpowder as a reality, therefore, did not exist, for they shied away from the concrete essence. If we carry this point further, that the use of gunpowder to kill is secondary, we can by symmetry say the use of medicine to cure is also secondary. What is primary is that it requires more humility of spirit to *find out about* a thing, than to decide this thing is evil, etc.

To find out about a thing is humbly to learn the shape of nature, which is also the will of God. I am inclining to the idea that sin cannot be identified until it be done, that an act becomes sin where it is identified as in conflict with the path to good, which is why we must sin before we can aspire to God, and why also a realism must be created before it is rejected (sense experience must come first, then we reject a sense experience for the greater knowledge).

This morning I ate eggs and bacon—not because I am giving up but because the diet of starches which I have been following is apparently responsible for my swollen neck, which is beginning to make swallowing difficult. Use of Citro carbonate helpful—last night and this morning yoga flat and unprofitable. Vivekananda says:

> Give up all argumentation and other distractions. Is there anything in *dry intellectual jargon?* It only throws the mind off balance and disturbs it. Things of subtler planes have to be realized. Will talking do that? So give up all vain talk. Read only those books which have been written by persons who have had realizations.

I confess I have not sufficiently given up. I might excuse the intellectual jargon (above) as trying to pull out certain minute perceptions. If I read, or look on the world, or indeed, sit and think, certain finer distinctions come up which I feel I should set down. In drawing them out they get wordy. "Those who really want to be Yogis must give up once and for all, this nibbling of things." Right.

October 6, 1946

The Mystic Will, Howard H. Brinton.

1. A little Boehme goes straight to the head. He speaks of the unspeakable and gives answers to the unanswerable. So we read Brinton with like enthusiasm. But then a second phase; it gets more complicated. We find we need Spinoza (1 reference), Hegel (12), Blake (10), Kant (10), Schopenhauer (18), Law (5), Whitehead, Eckhart (6), Bergson (4), Swedenborg (1), Treck (4), Spencer (1). Cancel Swedenborg, Spinoza, Spencer (only 1 each). So we end up with Hegel, Blake, Kant, Schopenhauer, etc.

Which isn't too much. But my point still holds. Too much intellection. Was Boehme a voluntaristic dualist or a rationalistic monist? Boop, boop a doop—lud sing coo-coo—lend me your handkerchief—

The unintelligible cry of the hawker in the street (selling Sunday papers) reminds us that we are dealing with realities—to which words are tickets. Now a "voluntaristic dualist" is a certain kind of ticket, let us say like an airline ticket; it has nothing to do with *where* you're going, except that it goes through Dedham. Also recall the ticket has to be checked—so really has a limited meaning. So the word dualist has a limited and rather unimportant meaning.

2. It is important to remember that the *Zeitgeist* of a new meaning such as the stimulus of the 4th dimension (Brunton, Ouspensky) or semantics (Korzybski, Chase) or Fort [Charles Fort, author of *Book of the Damned,* and other books on phenomena not explained by science, whose humor and philosophy I greatly admired] *has come* before. The illusion of new discovery of truth, the sense of opening doors, illumination, etc., is a *flavor,* a sensation. In the case of great writers of the past, age has made the flavor evaporate. A book that caused wars or burning at the stake is dry and sterile in an

historical account. Should we revive the flavor of the old, or remove the flavor of the new? I prefer the former. Why? Because we are obviously beyond rationalism. We are talking in a new way, about unspeakables.

3. So rather than take Brunton at his word (it is a little like a man writing about a picture) I would rather jump down into the bear pit with Boehme.

What is the lower ternary of Boehme?

Boehme	*Numerology*
1. Contraction, attraction, harshness, the magnet an impression. The principle of individuality and concrete being. The desire proceeding from the will and its creative fiat.	Number 1 is individuality, egoism— the self, the initiation.
2. Property of expansion. Centrifugal. It is the counter will. It makes pliable and movable—the sting of stirring— water spirit which softens or dissolves.	Number 2 is cooperation, softness, sensitivity, the wife of the god.
3. 1 + 2 do not cancel, they form what is the 3rd property of nature. Sensuality, bitter quality, struggle, strife, origin of distinction—it is rightful anguish.	Number 3 is creative, expressionistic art, beauty, etc.
4. The transition to freedom. Cross of self-denial. Entrance of Deity into nature. Birth of harmony.	Number 4 is composition, structure, construction, the right angle which makes possible the building, the combination of things.
5. Love—symbolized by the parable of the lotus.	Number 5 is curiosity, the breaking up of order by entrance of a new factor, the number of man (who tries to go beyond himself).

6. Sound, harmony, language.

Number 6—
Responsibility, family.

7. Consummation.

Number 7—Mystic
number.

October 7, 1946

It is now hardly possible to practice Yoga. In the morning there isn't time. At noon there is no place to go. In the evening I am tired. At midnight OK. I am still continuing the diet. The improvement in voice and poise has gone already. I find the plant as difficult as ever—and the longing for the new self returns.

Along this path I mention the Model 42, which is now torn apart, broken down. I hope that I will eventually help it; it would appear now that I've ruined it. I can act upon it only slowly, for so many others have their work to do on it—and so on. What am I? Am I the timid person I feel from present to present, hesitating on this and that? How can I have broken up this vast character [Model 42]—this which was such a great enterprise—how can I have done this unless the myself that extends through time is large too? Much larger than the one I am conscious of?

The Yoga has expired for the reasons mentioned before. I am more sick. Piles—neck swollen—a bad cold—I find plenty of new fuel—though the days are long, these crazed incidents flow away like dirty scraps of paper in the street caught up by a gust of wind, and I come home and sit.

I find the contemplation I have always done easier than Yoga —it is harder and no help to focus the eyes on the nose. The straight spine position no help either. Bart talked today about the quantum theory; it is amazing and quite similar to the logic of the Sutra. Identical things with identical velocities show scatter.

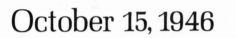

October 15, 1946

Worrying about Bell again. So I am slipping back into it. However, on the encouraging side I felt myself acting in an unattached manner yesterday, *i.e.,* doing the work for its own sake and ignoring justice. When I say justice I mean all those factors which one's pride, dignity, feeling of fairness rebel at. But I lost this when M. opposed the salary increase I've been trying to get for Bart.

November 11, 1946

Situation at Bell clear—at present. My understanding of why things have to be as they are is gradually seeping in and influencing my instinctive reactions and emotions. I am more able to act in a detached manner toward people. I can even watch them struggle. Nothing unique about this. It's just that this trend is becoming more firmly established in my natural habits.

I still hesitate to write, having a feeling that all I can say is mere intellection and wordiness. Today I caught myself getting

angry, frustrated, "going off in corner" when I could not get
Bart and Tom to understand my interpretation of the offset
blade. I throttled back. It worked. Their own antipathy melted.
Then they saw my point. Bell has become a laboratory in which
I try to distill myself. The helicopter is only the vessel.

November 18, 1946

For weeks now I've been taking out the furniture from the
house of my mind, pictures off the walls, rugs off the floor.
Now I see the dirt that was under the sofa, the light spot under
the pictures, the unpainted square under the rug. The rooms
seem no purer, only empty, the walls no less crowded; now
they remind one of what was once there—old vanities,
possessions, inheritances. What will fill their place? And I'm
full of a new fear that even the house must go, for an empty
house is cluttered with its emptiness—only a house full and
lived in is empty in the sense of Tao.

> Having so patiently crept through the wood,
>   and having seen at least the quarry
> I will not shout and fright the grazing deer
> Nor, when the wild swan settles on my lonely
>   swamp, scream it to heaven, and
>   discharge the gun, whose blast disrupts
>   the spell of evening, and at which
>   all nature stands aghast.

Went to show in Cleveland. Seeing the helicopters—Bell has
six, three inside and three flying—does not affect me at all. Even
seeing my designs copied by Sikorsky (tail rotor) does not. Yet
this is my child—down to the last detail. I seem rather to

consider the merits of the competitors and wonder if I've guessed right. [Two Model 47s were shown at the air show, the cabin model and the bubble model. It was the bubble that attracted attention.]

November 30, 1946

Through Hatha Yoga, etc., plus my own exploration I've developed a technique of exercising, developing, becoming aware of the spine. Bending it, stretching it, making it entirely loose (let your head roll around like a ball in a box—this is where we came in). The serpent feeds the appetite but at the same time stimulates it. A special stimulus, quasi-seminal, by putting one's knees against one's forehead—are these some form of magnetic currents?

The aches and pains in the back and legs have diminished. I am wondering whether Hatha is not my most natural path. I used to find a solution (in college) in gymnastics, especially tumbling, then having the conviction it was a matter of developing the spine. I remember how much importance I attached to the fact that without having practiced wrestling I could more than hold my own with the wrestling team, even with much heavier persons, because I had gained a strong back from tumbling. Part of the theory was that the back muscles were the foundation on which other links were attached, and that it was only necessary to develop the back, from which the strength would flow to the "accessories" as water flows into all the pipes from the main reservoir. Of course, this interest in athletics I finally suppressed by conscientiously abstaining from any form of exercise after I left college. During college, however, even at the Zen period, the daily gym session was the greatest portal to reality.

Now the question is, does this form of living fall in the category of sense experience, hence illusion?

December 2, 1946

Secrecy:

I feel I can break the silence. Some abstract ideas can be expressed. Mrs. Forman showed me something from a Theosophical magazine about secrecy—importance of it, etc.

I was completely in agreement as to the reasons for secrecy, which are the ordinary ones such as not telling people who would not appreciate it, etc., plus one I figured out myself, which has many forms, *i.e.,* a spectrum from "truth inverts if it is expressed" to "the explanation of an act deflates it." But there are valid reasons *against* secrecy, which are:

1. Harboring a secret prevents its digestion and growth. It should be pulled apart, and developed—open discussion does this. For this reason a secretive attitude is bad for a scientific approach, or for the inventor.

2. The fencing in of secrets has the effect of keeping our attention on what we have and fencing out possible new truths.

3. A presumptuous attitude is fostered in the inventor—to preserve a secret, he *presumes* he does not need to know more. This is apparent to anyone who listens to a certain kind of inventor talk about his invention. This attitude of secrecy prevents his learning important facts.

Since that discussion, which was last night, it now occurs to me that I might go even further. While I confined the antisecrecy to science, it is possible that it applies to the esoteric as well. Maybe that's what's wrong with the world today. If there is a mental science of great import, people should know it. People today have lost their respect for their fellowman, for *man* himself. Perhaps if they knew more about man, that he is capable of great power, their respect would return, their humility would return. The decay of religion is because religion does not command respect any more. It is all very well for a few enlightened ones, who know that man is capable of unlimited power, to have the due humility, but such people we might say don't need correction.

A further reason appears when we consider what it is that has given science its great impetus and strength today. More than any one factor I would say it was communication. The laws of science have been the common property of civilization. Science began when people began to communicate.

Reading Kammerer: *Inheritance of Acquired Characteristics.* [This is the book which Koestler refers to in *The Case of the Midwife Toad.*]

1. The basic error of science in dealing with the body is to deal with it as a piece of machinery. Machinery is properly analyzed as a combination of *separate* parts, whereas a living organism is *one thing* having no parts whatever. (*Viz.,* the wheel is a part of a machine, it is intrinsically separate from the rest of a machine. There is no way the machine could build or repair its own wheel because to do so it would have to transport something across the boundary of the wheel, in this case the bearing surface, which, since the wheel rotates, had to be entirely separate from the axle on which it rotates. A living organism is connected with all its parts, even a tooth has nerves that communicate with the brain, etc., etc.)

2. Such ideas as the "immutability of species" are also carryovers of this habit of analysis.

3. Recognized for what it (life) really is, *i.e.,* one thing, a unit, not a combination of related parts, it then is but a short step to many of the basic precepts of mentalism, etc. (cultivation of the consciousness, its extraordinary powers, etc., etc.). Why? Because since life is one thing, it has a central directing agency. This cannot be the brain, but the brain can be "put in touch with" the other. Superconsciousness could be such.

I feel exceptionally well recently—full of whatever it is. It may be due to Raja Yoga, or just the periodicity of mood, but I attribute it to Hatha Yoga, which makes my blood sing and my spine glow. After a protracted period of sexual abstinence I have now relinquished the veil. (I took it only on the condition that my thoughts were pure, which they were until recently.)

Certainly the spine is the foundation of all athletic activity. Perhaps it is also so for all nervous activity, by which we import the control of the whole being.

December 12, 1946

Larry Bell said yesterday about the Air Show that the people who went to it went like people go to the zoo to see the giraffe, not to buy one. He has this mastery of imagery that always commands my respect.

I've spilled over to Bart a little about how to bring about the desired attitude toward the helicopter at the plant, by not interceding between wrong action and its retribution, by not telling people what they should do, not snatching the opportunity of working out a problem by presenting the answer. Had I been better under control I would not have "explained" to him. His comment was, it sounds as though you'd been reading *How to Win Friends and Influence People.* Must be careful. See how the force of the idea is made static by "explaining" it. Explanation isolates it and makes it a target instead of an influence. If I can contribute anything, it is the recognition of the working of this subtle, simple law: that which is unexpressed is dynamic, active.

There is now a Sikorsky R-5 in the hangar consigned to us for tests. This contrasts glaringly with our own helicopters. It is of a totally different species. As an object of contemplation, it helps make my own an object of contemplation. The fish seeing the bird begins to know he is a fish.

After a period of not looking at what was going on at Bell I went around with Bart today and feel rather discouraged. . . . There remains a fundamental blindness, a refusal on

management's part to face the issue or see what it is necessary
to see. It seems that the lessons we've learned have to be
learned all over again. And I can conjure up only philosophy,
not tolerance or rebuke in answer. I'm afraid Bart feels that the
philosophy is not the proper answer.

So far as the rebuke answer is concerned, this would be as
futile as telling children not to throw snowballs. There is a kind
of childish enthusiasm—an absence of the faculty of accepting
anything from outside. This appears to be a function of
the novelty of the thing. For example, the 42 had this same
treatment until its complete collapse, after which no one would
touch it with a ten-foot pole and the separate groups started to
swarm all over the 47.

What will happen? The trouble is that the answer is far off.
Months will elapse before the effect of acts now made will be
felt and when these results occur no one will be there to learn
the lesson. Who would learn it, anyway?

An example of how difficult it is to keep score:

It was determined theoretically that we would get greater
speed with long blades. At great expense production was
changed to provide them. Finally they were ready. Time after
time I requested a comparative test. Tests were made (to
determine highest speed possible with short and long blades). A
great deal of data was prepared, but due to airspeed calibration,
malfunctioning engine, incomplete test, etc., the answer was not
forthcoming. There exists to this moment no conclusive test or
combination of tests to show either the comparative high speed
or the difference in speed. To get such tests requires a very
strong will, which is lacking in the "organization"—hence the
result never occurs. To supply this will oneself discourages its
growth in others. Hence I am torn between wanting to get the
answer and wanting others to want. Perhaps the answer is that
we can never know positively where we stand. We live on, not
asking too many questions, surrounding ourselves with a
complicated frame of delusion which we do not expose because
it doesn't matter. A sign says "no exit" so we never open the
door. So an actual score is very rare. We don't know what the
gas mileage is on our car. It is within the tolerance, so we don't
measure it.

What am I beefing about? What should management do, etc?

Simply this. Recognize the helicopter for what it is and organize the manufacture around the product and the people who know how to make it. I suppose that this is what we are gradually coming to, but by such a slow and painful process that I grow discouraged. Bart's instance is the forward landing gear. He had a simple way to do it which involves very slight changes. It was decided not to do it because it could not be incorporated by September of this year when first deliveries were to be made. It is now December and no deliveries have been made yet on any landing gear. Meanwhile the production engineering department has made a new design for which parts cannot be made until next March, and even this does not allow for a trial installation. Another of Bart's examples is the transmission test fixture. The one for the 48 cost $30,000 so far and is still not working. The one for the 47 cost $2,000 and is in operation—an example of the greater efficiency of letting the people who know do the job.

One would think that these lessons would take effect. But there does not appear to be any keeping of the score. It seems to me that blunders multiply and obfuscation covers them up.

Where is my error? The story is the same as it has always been. I have tried to teach myself to let things work themselves out, which was all right, but there are two objections. The money may run out first, and no one is around to learn the lessons.

I register another. For years I've been requesting good people to learn by doing. Now we are coming to the end. Soon the 42, which had been turned over to me to fix, will be done (only the engine mount and the body shape remain). When this is done, there will be no more opportunity to teach how to make a helicopter work. So the next model will have no one to nurse it through. Perhaps the answer is that we won't need any more models. We will have our ship of illusions with painted portholes, and in this we will live until competition puts forth a better one. We will still continue on our initial inertia, even after the soundings begin to show shallow water and end at last with a scraping of the bottom, a shudder, and finally a great sliding of movable furniture, the piano coasting across the floor—grounded on a spit of sand. The Coast Guard will rescue the passengers but the old ship will just groan and toss, beaten by surf and tide.

December 13, 1946

Today I looked out the window of the plant. Ship 3B was hovering motionless against the high clouds. I felt the wonder of it and thought how, when clouds were especially impressive, I would see a helicopter against them, rotor turning, but the machine without motion. It was false to think that this was my dream. It is the dream that many dream, and I have walked on it as on a field of wheat. Who is the farmer who planted the wheat? I do not know. But more and more people are climbing over the fence now.

December 24, 1946

Reading the Gita.

The distinction between matter and spirit.

Imagine trying to create consciousness.

The simplest life a self-enlarging and dividing cell.

I recollect the conference about helicopter problems at Bell when I was able to be a disinterested spectator and see them sitting on the raft of the helicopter idea—some rowing, some steering, some observing, but the variety was in the people, the unity in the idea.

When of differences there are many, of oneness there is one.

The difference between materialism and Hinduism is in the

solubility of consciousness. In the former we have elements
accepted as real, combining to form higher realms, creating
"effects." These are real in their own realms. So a'oms create
chemical substances which affect each other chemically.
Chemical substances create organic matter, organisms. The latter
are real to each other (on the subjective level). The reality of
these realms is transitory (can be destroyed) except for the
lowest realm. And now we have even that subject to
dissolution. Consciousness then must be transitory. For the
Hindu, all is the field of consciousness. Consciousness is not
transitory but more permanent than its content, which includes
all matter.

Naturally, the hasty interpretation of mentalism as intending
that electrons are dream stuff, nonexistent, is untenable, but that
consciousness can be a "substance" (by which I mean something
having reality, although unmanifest, etc.) pervading even the
atom is not untenable at all. Put it this way: Electrons feel force,
force builds itself into what we call consciousness, consciousness
through Nirvana unknots itself, rolls back and becomes simple,
hence not dependent on combination (life).

December 29, 1946

Life is not very satisfactory but it is good enough to keep me
from losing it. I went Friday to Swami Yatiswarananda, who
gave me an interview. He emphasized the subject of meditation.
Think of the self, what is it? I kept saying there must be a
discipline, a technique, which he could impart. He attached no
importance to this—put emphasis on what we think, not so
much how. Sounded like Steiner. "Think of the lotus of the
heart, it is lighted with a glow." Yesterday I tried to think of the
self that was always beside me, never in me—a brown man who
pushed my ego, cut out of flat paper, against the wall. My ego

had printed in black and white, "ego," "ego," "ego," but the brown man was wordless.

The Cloud of Unknowing says that love, not knowing, is the way. I recollected my justification to myself for the study of mysticism. For I always revert to my true career, which I call the discovery of the processes of the mind. And if this pursuit should take me into religion and by religion I was to become critical of my original plans, by virtue of my having been smaller than religion would have made me become, this would be unfortunate. Yet not really so either. The stock answer would be that if in taking up religion as a subject for science one went religious, it was because religion was greater than science (the scientifically inclined would say the man entered dotage). That's the stock answer—what I say is that I have faith in my original plan (I assume that the authority that placed me on a certain course was a higher one) and if the plan seems to involve me in "temptations" that swerve me from the original purpose—this is all part of the plan and must be gone through. We may say The Cloud of Unknowing would banish knowing as a means to God, so the original plan could not be carried out. Such criticism is queasy, trivial. The card entitles one to pass the door; do not therefore become employed in argument with the doorkeeper. There is a way of knowing; it denies knowing. But logic can also deny knowing—as it has already denied loving.

January 1, 1947

As I looked out the window of my father's studio, full of a sense of the beauty of nature in his marine paintings, I wondered how it was transferred, or caught. This is also love—love of nature—a positive feeling of hunger—there is even some question whether it is without an object (Zen and myself have distinguished between emotions craving an object of satisfaction and those on a "higher" aesthetic plane). The distinction may be arbitrary too, but the voice of experience tells me this emotion, this hunger, must be trained, disciplined, if it is to accomplish anything.

What does this mean? I am thinking of the epistemology of the thing. We start out infantlike to touch the fire. We burn our fingers. We learn at last "how to go about it." We wish to fly. We dream of flight. We strap wings to our back and jump off a roof and fall flat on our face. Then we go back to the attic and labor, years of painful pushing and withdrawing, finally to emerge, humbled, beset with conditions, burdened with specifications, with a rocket airplane, more visions, more terrible than any dream, more wonderful, too—and scarcely look to see it launched. What is trained? What has happened? Has the *élan vital* been trimmed and controlled, or is the *élan* still a wild seeking, forcing itself through a barrier of natural, legal, and human obstructions?

My question is then, How is the *élan* modified? Or is it modified? Is this the control the Hindu speaks of? We learn to do something. To get to Europe, to write for rooms, to govern our emotion—yet we never cease to crave that direct outlet, to sit down at the piano and reel off the perfect sonata, to lash out with the brush and catch the elusive magic of nature, to open the spigot of imagination and pour forth divinest poesy. Even simpler, I find myself yearning for a form of physical activity that will not require so much control, where I can let myself go.

Stuck with myself.

The elimination of the helicopter leaves me with a sort of wallflower feeling. Admittedly, I am suddenly faced with a barren vista. The strong interest has not failed me. I am constantly directing myself toward attainment of the psychopter —mingled with the distraction of the new self, which is a physical need as well as a spiritual ambition, so it is hard to put aside. The idea that it must for practical reasons be put aside vies with the parallel rationalization that it is my last fling on earth—one which I have to complete—a karma.

Filling out the questionnaire for the Princeton twenty-year Yearbook is like burying a dead dog. How small—it doesn't even take much of a hole.

January 2, 1947

Drove out to Bell alone.

I now have the feeling that this morning brought some perceptible progress.

First, I was conscious of the sin of envy and anger and perhaps sloth.

For, from *The Cloud of Unknowing:*

> . . . in so much that if it be a thing which grieveth or hath grieved thee before, there riseth in thee a painful passion and an appetite of vengeance—the which is called Anger— or else a full disdain and a manner of loathing of their persons with despiteful and condemning thoughts, the which is called Envy—or else a weariness, and an unlistness of any good occupation bodily or ghostly—the which is called Sloth.

Perhaps not so much sloth.

So I should not feel as I do toward many of the people at Bell.

Second, I despaired of stating anything in words.

Third, I reflected on how much I would welcome death.

There were other conditions. I kept reminding myself that I must give up my love for ice cream, for my new self, not because it was wrong but because it was the wrong place to put this attachment.

I had to get the tire fixed so I waited in the gas station. My mind said, "You should plan more efficiently, so that you don't waste time waiting in gas stations." To which I answered, "What difference? A gas station is as good a place to think as any other. All I have to do now is think."

Take a principle such as *truth reverses when it is stated.* Here is
something that is true—and it obeys the litmus test that it be
unusable. A gyro has some of this property. It responds in a
direction other than that in which it is pushed. Looking in a
mirror, one sees everything backward, and one must reverse 180
degrees.

The mind which sees the world combatively must do a
reversal when it seeks truth.

Then I thought about women. First you must learn to give
flowers, then you must learn not to give flowers. You may
indulge in passion if you don't want to, is the rule. *(Viz.,* the
shipboard incident in *Brideshead Revisited.)*

Then I reflected that I should write a book on the helicopter.
The pattern of a vice is not a vice if you don't crave it. It was
seductively beckoning me on. What is the difference between
attaining a long-sought goal, and attaining a nondesire for the
goal?

Through the Hindoo windoo
or How do you do a helicopter

> Why you do and you undo, then you do and you undo,
> then you do, then you begin voodoo, so you do until you
> do everything—when you see everything you have to do by
> this time you don't care what you do.

Then I drove on. Many thoughts went skimming along with
me as I drove through the slush; as I passed the Huntley Station
I decided to stop and write some down:

> There is the fable of the fox who took out insurance in case
> he should have to be like the polar bear. He was a good
> provider. He was also worried about what would happen if
> he were to have to make his own living, like the polar bear
> who had to live at the North Pole and catch fish by
> swimming in the Arctic water (the fox felt guilty about
> stealing farmers' chickens). So he took a course at the
> university and finally went up north for special training.

How to attain the higher life? Is it the same as coming to
believe that it doesn't exist? Perhaps (like the love of women

and doing the helicopter) in being in it we would not see it. The Zen Buddhist says act on impulse, but impulse merges into Karma again.

The intellectual quandary I am in, the muddle, is not worse than any beginner's, not worse than I was when I learned to drive a car, not worse than the man who, having been wounded, has to learn again to walk—to use his hands.

Maybe I'm wrong about renouncing Bell. Maybe the thing I seek is there, there in the confused muddle, the torture of dull and stupid conferences, in the patience required waiting for the light to dawn. Maybe it's there in taking up the sword and cutting off their heads, doing battle with standard weapons. The only answer to that is: the best sword is the poison the enemy eats from his own dish.

So I wriggle out with the claim that I wait for this poison to take effect.

January 7, 1947

Coming home I talked with Bart and Dave about the problem of reality—the need for a subjective view to answer this metaphysical question. What force prevented the electron falling into the nucleus? To understand these things we should deal with what we know, *i.e.,* people—we can have only objective inference about electrons. They shied at this. Bart is reading the Gita. He commented on the lack of discussion in modern physics about the uniformity of mass or charge on the electron. He wanted to show it could be considered a probable mass, etc. The idea that mass has the uniqueness of an event. (You can't buy an ice cream soda 1 1/2 times.)

I had a more successful meditation (reduced exercise to a minimum), and again that evening after some visitors left, but still not much more than a feeling (of being suspended). (The conversation of our guests turned around the younger-generation parties where it has become customary to turn out the lights.)

This feeling in my lower end, which has been with me on and off for three weeks, is similar to that fear you feel when you buy a house, or take some large step. It seems to be a welling up of fluid to float a vast and newly constructed ship; it conveys to the mind a sense of fear. I say it is a pleasant dread, for now it is in the main agreeable.

January 13, 1947

Went to see Swami Bodenanda, who had been Vivekananda's disciple. He wore a rather unkempt costume of a faded sweater and old trousers. He complained of race prejudice in America. People thought he was a colored man. I asked, Didn't Buddha teach this should be ignored? If a man spits in your face you should be unmoved by it. Yes, he said, but this man must be punished. . . . Had he attained Samadhi? (He said he'd worked on Yoga fifty years.) No, but he believed in it. I kept thrusting back the impulse to judge him, thinking it would disturb our conference. He said there were three things he was glad of. He was unmarried; he never worked for money; I forget the third. We discussed Bragdon. He kept trying to use science as his support. (I had told him I worked on the helicopter.) When he talked about the fourth dimension I said that Bragdon had lifted the term from Relativity where it has a special technical meaning, but used the color of the word to support rather vague ideas. He misunderstood my word color, started to talk about the color of emotions (à la Steiner). I asked if I might smoke but he said not to smoke in this room which was their chapel.

His attitude partook of the poor priest. There seemed to be no intellectual grasp. Most of his conversation was directed at the low level of intelligence of the people he was converting. I gathered he was rather discouraged.

I decided to try Mr. Williamson, the teacher of Yoga, whom both Mrs. Forman and Gretchen Green had recommended. He made room for me. (He had a letter from Mrs. Forman.) He showed me just how to do the exercises. Talked a lot about the significance, said I was very tense, showed me new exercises, was quite intelligent.

He said Sikorsky had made a number of appointments but had not kept them.

January 17, 1947

Yesterday I cracked up in the 42. Ship turned over while attempting to taxi around in a pretty stiff wind. The threat of death was not convincing. The idea that it might be the end was rather welcome—but it wasn't the end. Not a scratch. I felt that evening the need for greater excitement.

January 22, 1947

The purpose of the notes is as a diary and as a wall on which to bounce the tennis balls.

Another purpose is actually as a laboratory (*i.e.,* in double talk, cipher, poetry).

January 23, 1947

Meditation at breakfast. Looking in my notes for a date of
conception (3B rotor, December 27, 1944), I was impressed
by the intensity and concentration of purpose manifested.
One-pointedness. This is what made the helicopter successful.
Am I not now too scattered, too diverse? I answered myself,
saying, no, this is all the psychopter, these are all aspects of an
effort to sever the mind from its moorings. Some are not
contributory. We must sift out the chaff.

January 30, 1947

Plan:
    I have enough evidence to indicate that concentration and/or
breathing is the most effective technique. I have therefore
reaffirmed the program.
    Half-hour Hatha Yoga, breathing, and concentration:
    1. Before breakfast—necessary now to wake at 6:30.
    2. At noon—if possible.
    3. Before dinner—get home 5:45–6:00,
                    nap to 6:15–6:30.
    Exercise 20 minutes. Breathing—10.
                    Concentrate—10.
    4. Midnight.

I let the breathing and concentration lapse lately in favor of the easier Hatha exercises, to the detriment of mind. I'm now recognizing need for restraint on the exercises, which have brought me very good health and well-being but should not displace more important and much more difficult mental drill.

Minds:
A monk asked Joshu, "What is the one ultimate word of truth?" Joshu replied, "Yes."
Another monk asked another master the same question. The reply was, "You make it two."
"What is myself?" "What would you do with a self?"
"What is Tao?" "Usual life is very Tao."
"How can we accord with it?" "If you try to accord with it, you will get away from you."
"Deny nothing. Affirm all."
"I am not yet I am."
"The mind is the slayer of the real."
The future does not come from before to meet us: it comes steaming (streaming) up from behind over our heads.
An Indian prince gave a ring to his jeweler and asked him to engrave in it a sentence that would support him in adversity and restrain him in prosperity. The jeweler engraved therein this sentence—"It will pass."

Definite proof of Hatha Yoga's efficacy. I did a handstand on an armchair from a seated position with great ease. This was difficult even twenty years ago. I have not tried it for at least ten years.
Mrs. Forman said I'm expecting results too quickly. Look at the tree, she said.
Went to the zoo Saturday again. C. says I should paint animals. (So far I've only drawn them.)

February 5, 1947

Zoo Monday. Brought watercolors.

Plant Tuesday. A good day mocking up a body for the coaxial. Have not flown it yet. Bad weather, but everything now works OK. Changed to single carburetor this week.

I am trying harder on concentration. Get at least 10 minutes plus 10 minutes breathing plus about 10–30 minutes Hatha three times a day but the jump of progress noted a week ago did not develop any further. Nor have my efforts to carry consciousness over into sleep been successful, although now and then I have hints.

To break through the screen—is it those silent flashes of heat lightning across the back side of the shell of mind, is that the goal? More and more there are murmurings from the out of focus. An invisible waitress is putting the plates of food on the table before us.

Am I what I always was? It seems to me I sit here, the same identity that I was with my first recollections. My memory takes me back to childhood but I sense no difference. I feel the same as I did then for all the puttering that I've done in the room.

> Oh inscrutable face of morning,
> the light falls again on your stone eyes—
> the warm sun plays across your cheek,
> can you not give me a wink of recognition,
> must I always bash my weak hands
> on your iron gate?
> Oh imperturbable inevitable day,
> how can you hold yourself so serene,
> move with such inevitable force in one direction?

Sometimes I rush to meet you,
sometimes I swerve to avoid the collision,
always you advance with inevitable
yet imperceptible speed, always to engulf me,
so that I find myself in your middle,
thrashing like a swimmer in the surf,
and when I am about to go under
suddenly find myself lying on the
sandy beach of evening, exhausted,
with no fight left. I look up,
the light is fading,
you are vanishing into the evening.

How many times have you passed me thus? Still you will
give me no nod of recognition.

When I look back on machines, or see gadgets in the store
windows, or hear of new devices, I feel bored with mechanical
things, I think that our new inventions must be with living
things—with life. What about all the people going in the
opposite direction, selling helicopters to each other? Well, let
them go. I detect a new feeling in the air, a wave of revulsion
against things mechanical. Now for me it is life. The crane at the
zoo, a live mouse in his bill, washed him, gave him a few bites,
then swallowed him head first. I'm sure the mouse was still
alive.

About concentration:
No progress; still have to make a great effort of will to keep
my mind on the point. Now it's the dot on the A in the word
"safety" on the match box. If the dot were a glass of water I
was holding on my eye beam, I could not cross the room
without dropping it. In fact, I looked across the room and
dropped it without a clatter of broken glass.

But to hell with progress. I do it—I will go on doing it. If
progress comes, can spring be far behind? Bragdon must have
been doing Yoga for forty years, as must Bodenanda, and there
couldn't have been much progress.

However, I think that concentration is the very heart of
action. If one can concentrate, one can do. I should try bowling,

or dart throwing. If, as I read recently, imagining one is throwing darts improves the aim as rapidly as really throwing them, then concentrating on a point would be equally good, and would provide universal practice. Certain things I seem to be doing better as a result of concentration. Painting the coaxial body—but to hell with progress.

February 6, 1947

Ruses, I am so full of ruses. For example, people ask me why I don't have a license to fly my own helicopter. I say I wish to keep my inability to fly so as to retain a fresh view. The pilots get used to a ship and become immune to its faults. But this is a ruse. Because I am somewhat afraid of flying I feel I must manufacture a reason for not doing it. That is not the reason, either, however. I am not interested in flight. I am interested in the problem. When the thing works, I lose interest. Reasoning that I'm not interested in flying because I fear it is false, because this makes me fly more than I would if I didn't fear it, etc. Reasoning that I'm not interested in flying because I'm not interested in a thing that works is valid, because as soon as something doesn't work, my interest takes a new spurt.

So much for the example. Let us go on to the work at hand. I am interested now in the psychopter—because it won't work. What is the psychopter.

The psychopter is the winged self. It is that which the helicopter usurped—and what the helicopter was finally revealed not to be.

The psychopter is the will to be unchained from the laws of nature, and to venture into the unknown. We expect that when it returns it will carry a message. It will establish laws of the mind (Theory of Structure and Process). Why should an exponent of liberty turn to law-making? What a question. Well, it is asked, and it can be answered but the answer is only *an* answer, and the shell of *the* answer.

To be free of the laws we must know what they are. That is the role of consciousness. The seeker of liberty should make laws, because he must have freedom to overstep boundaries. When you ask, what message will he bring, you budget the quest. The answer might be "throw everything away!" Where then would your anticipation be? Perhaps you are smart; you say, "If that is the answer, I will liquidate my stock holdings." But that is not it. The clank of your medals will draw the wolves.

So this quest may be settled right here. *We cannot be wise.* If the Zen philosopher ends with his enlightenment in reembracing the suchness of things, if he says "ordinary life is very Tao," it does not mean that he returns to a state of noneffort. So *we cannot be stupid.*

In the circle of conscious development negation of negation is not the same as assertion. The important thing is that the circle misses returning into itself. It accelerates in a new direction; namely, up out of the plane of the paper. There is no solution in the plane of the combat. The battle rages, the bodies fall. It is the smoke that rises.

Suzuki says that intellection is Zen's worst enemy. Or it was. Is this true—still? For intellection is our only tool. I cannot solve this problem. I have to say that intellection (which can wipe out its own footprints with a cloth) is the only salvation. Otherwise, the stone is the highest philosopher.

The Zen Koàn and the act of its realization appears to have a resemblance to the dream. That is, in the dream one is in a state where either:

1. The critical faculty is so low that ideas lead into one another without injunction by the rational process. That's rather poorly expressed. Ideas, that in the waking state are unrelated, are permitted to follow one another, because the critical faculty is asleep. Or

2. There is a higher relatedness. That is, in sleep some higher faculty perceives a connectedness.

This poses the question, "If the critical faculty is a negative faculty, then is its absence equivalent to the presence of a positive faculty?"

It is as though children were crossing the ice. They leap from point to point without concern about falling through. The parent cautions them, says "no" at each step. The adult bases his "no" on consciousness or memory of danger. "Fools rush in," etc. It happened yesterday with the helicopter, Model 42, when Tr. and several other visitors came and flew the machine much more recklessly than our own pilots would dare to. I also note with myself an absence of the feeling of dread with the Sikorsky ship because I'm not aware of its weaknesses. I have less feeling of dread in turn with the 42 than with the 47 because the latter I know very intimately. On the whole it is certainly more sensible to say that the critical faculty is a "positive" thing, consisting of *positive* consciousness of adverse or negative effects. (Painting or any technique is knowing what *not* to do.)

Reading Dunne, *Experiment with Time.*

His theory suggests an even more general one: that everything is composed of pieces of experience and a dream. *Viz.,* the Model 47 is comprised of pieces of model experience, plus sailboat models (from 1913–1917).

February 11, 1947

With breakfast dish pushed back
Begins in contemplation rapt the day.

Reading the Koan yesterday to R. "Like a dog beside a boiling grease pot—he cannot touch it, yet he cannot go away." Like a rat trapped in the corner of a barn, he has to be really stuck before he goes all the way round.

I have two Koans. Bell and my new self. I have solved neither. But we should cease to think of the world as nonverbal. Just because we can picture a relationship does not mean we can get out of it. If we could objectify it clearly enough, we could perhaps. The question of the reality of an object, say an automobile, is bound up in the question of whose automobile it is.

February 12, 1947 (5:30A.M.)

Dream fragment: I looked out the window at Radnor and saw where a snow plow had endeavored to plow the drive. Not knowing where it was, however, they made a straight line from the gate to the house with a circle in the middle.

At plant (evening the same day): There was a snow plow at Bell. I went over to examine it. The operator was an old friend. I looked down from a platform on the snow plow whose screw drove snow onto a conveyor which carried it back and up. The incident was sufficiently similar that, had I seen the plow first, I would have attributed the dream to it.

February 13, 1947

Dunne's theory is borne out by the above. Do you hear me? I said I have found Dunne's theory correct, *i.e.,* that *we dream of the future as well as of the past.* [At this time I was reading Dunne's *Experiment with Time,* in which he describes his own experience with precognitive dreams. The dream fragment about the snow plow was my first experience of what Dunne calls "future resemblance." It made a great impression on me. Shortly before this I had noticed that some of the thoughts which interrupted my concentration exercise were *hypnagogic images* which I later found were sometimes precognitive.]

Blavatsky has the gods creating reality to see how it works— which is the fundamental reason I took up the helicopter, to act out a real experience, to do some actual thing (in Time 1 as Dunne calls it). Thus the mind lacks the discrimination that the brain gives it. The Hindus describe a higher learning where discrimination is laid aside, but this discrimination is necessary, as forming the matter (or body) of thought.

About the importance of several value scales corresponding to the several time scales. The market value being the real value, etc. Dunne's method challenges materialists and spiritualists alike in defining "the observer at infinity," which is our waking self.

The Moral: Dunne has shown once again the truth that has been pregnant in my mind, ready to drop, separate out: You must think through or live through every crook and cranny, that nothing can pass by, everything must go through the mill. Examples:

1. Every shelved puzzle of the helicopter returns soon or later to haunt us. Until a particular part is sweat-covered it will not rest but will rise again. Latest is the throttle.

2. My attitude toward not learning to fly is coming nearer to being explained. I have this feeling that I must live in the state of learning to keep the right attitude, a sort of respect which is necessary if I am to serve. A butler could not be a good butler if he had an affair with his mistress.

3. With mathematics it is the same. I cultivate a state of puzzlement. I do not want to master the mathematics. I want to deal with the state of puzzlement. Example: The problem of how much flapping a given amount of feathering induces can be solved simply. I preferred to make it an infinite series. Naively but forcefully, I pushed through the much more general problem of what makes an infinite series have a limit. Such energy was required before the mathematical technique was invented and

made it unnecessary. But the thought pattern involved is much the same as Dunne employs in his idea of serial time. My energy as applied to time might have come up with Dunne's solution; in other words, the business of thinking through is still necessary, for the problems which beset us have not been solved. Mathematics just snatches away the lower rungs of the ladder of reason.

4. My relation to my Koans. First the new self, with standard apologies for the possibility of error. I think I have solved it. We deal with a relation between A and B. B says it is "just b." A says if so, then A is just an a. Then the relation AB is just ab. ab is finite; therefore AB is finite. The Bell one is not solved. How is this an example? Because it is a thinking through.

5. All the Chinese Koans are objects for concentration. In Christian mysticism the Godhead takes the place of the Koan. It might be that this intense concentration is related to the possibility of establishing T_2 or some other time as a time to exist in and defeat the cessation of T_1. I suppose this is Dunne's theory.

Thursday—Painted watercolor of Tonawanda across Niagara River on way to plant. Afternoon at plant. Time with C. C. Torque propeller difficulties.

February 20, 1947

As I look back on it I had a rather curious day. Especially in the afternoon I felt different—principally due to the step I've taken with regard to the new self, which so far as I am concerned is to give it up. Though as far as everything else is concerned there might be no change, which is equivalent to giving up the old self that has been looking on the new self as something to be possessed by it (I am tempted to add that the reverse is more likely).

In other words I don't feel the identity of myself. The experience of walking about the plant, going to see different people to hear their troubles showed me I no longer cared what was my own and what was not my own. The great organic throbbing problem (of the helicopter) was on everyone's mind. The same difficulties, the same struggle, involved us all. Everyone has the capacity to learn, to come to the same conclusion eventually because of having lived through the same evolution.

Recently I've felt a sort of martyr to having lost—a failure to have achieved what I should have wanted but didn't. Perhaps a failure to want—at any rate a feeling of not getting something I should have had. It was as though at a children's party I saw children who had no ice cream, but realized I myself wanted not to eat ice cream (not didn't want ice cream).

One thing that made me a little conscious of this—for the feeling did not carry the consciousness of it with it; it is as though I now look back on a dream—was that Bart spoke of my calmness and detachment, said that it must be a result of my practices. The statement rather surprised me because I was not aware of anything other than my usual struggle to attain this state.

The sequence that led to not wanting:

Giving up sex—giving up abstinence from sex.

Hundreds of conscious efforts at the plant to forego tasting of personal triumph.

Giving up cigarettes. This is one of the most important.

Making myself do exercises, breathing, and concentration.

Making myself wake up and write down dreams.

Giving up my new self.

February 23, 1947

Dream:

In a theater after a lot of build-up, a nude girl climbs up on a wooden curtain and becomes impaled at the center of the curtain high up. She remains there almost upside-down. The next act continues the suspense, but this curtain is not let down. After other false starts, a new scene appears with a sort of mail slot in the same spot where the impaled girl was. . . .

February 26, 1947

Last night Priscilla and I went to the theater. Tallulah Bankhead in *The Eagle Has Two Heads*. The last act ends with her going up some stairs back stage. As she gets to the top of the stairs, she is shot by the hero. With difficulty she continued. At the French window at the head of the stairs, she grabs the curtain, falls back and partly down the stairs still holding the curtain; her head down, her legs up. This ends the play.

I saw the curtain scene about 11:00 P.M. last evening. I was not conscious of the resemblance to the dream at the time. Backstage, we stood outside the door of Miss Bankhead's dressing room. After waiting about fifteen minutes, I left a note inviting her to take a ride in the helicopter.

[Since I'd written down the dream before I saw the play, I had convincing evidence of what Dunne reported in *Experiment with Time.* It could not be dismissed as chance because it was unusual; one doesn't expect to see a woman upside down on the stage. Apart from Freudian interpretations, the mail slot in the dream must refer to my leaving the note.]

February 28, 1947

Two of my friends have reported dreams with future resemblances.

Martha dreamed of being in a hospital. There was much washing of blood. Physicians washing their hands, a pretty nurse in attendance. She told us this dream at the Tennis Club February 22; it had occurred two nights before.

That very night as they left the Club, she and Doc saw a drunk lying in the snow, his head covered with blood. They took him to a hospital. Martha washed her hands which had become covered with blood. She looked up—there was a pretty nurse in attendance.

G. told me yesterday, February 27, of a dream she had had that morning. She was sitting in the street. Suddenly there was a terrific noise. Some boards fell down beside her. That day at art school she was conducting a class. Suddenly there was a terrific noise just outside the window where she was standing. Some boards fell from the new wing being added to the art school. She was electrified and said aloud, "My God, this is terrible!" Later a student inquired the cause of her alarm—it turned out he knew of Dunne or something based on Dunne.

We must hammer our data into the data box. Helicopter data have become increasingly contradictory of late. Principally because there is no one to "hammer the data into place." I was the cause. Generally, the wandering data turn out to be explainable when "there is a motive for" making them keep their place. One has to shepherd one's data. This does not necessarily mean that all data are false or fiction (as Fort would have it). There is still a higher meaning, which even Fort would find.

March 2, 1947 (7:00 A.M.)

Hypnagogic images (during concentration exercises):
Statue of Pan on a leaf. . . . Vitrification in two Italian cities.
. . . The view of Italian towns—cathedral (1) . . . The spy carriage (woman and two men) . . . What's the matter with your hand? . . . The movers—the large camera with the 5-inch lens (9 × 12) . . . The waiting line for lunch (college) (2) . . . Being carried around on someone's shoulders . . . Missing the transmission wires (3) . . . The man shouldn't change the light bulb while touching the wires . . . He is careful not to . . . I tell how carefully insulated the circuits are (not grounded).
March 2, 1947 (same day)
(After spending the day at Murray Hill skiing: Several of the above images had resemblance to actual events that happened later during the day.)
1. Looking at *Life* magazine this evening. Picture of Siena Cathedral.
2. A waiting line for lunch at the Murray Hill Ski Club.
3. I took a walk in the deep snow at Murray Hill. I twice crossed wires—once an electric fence, again a barbwire fence. The feeling of elevation due to the deep snow similar to being

carried on someone's shoulders. Had to step on the wire as I crossed it.

The feeling that life is ended continues. Reading Lakavantra Sutra (Suzuki, Vol. 4). On my walk at Murray Hill and after— the ominousness of having dreams of the future. *I want to scream about it,* but people continue to keep their eyes on the ground.

March 4, 1947

An incident occurred at the plant. Several times now I've heard of them having to tear ships down to change the oil seal at the top of the transmission. I heard myself say to the pilot who told me how many ships this was happening to, sometimes over and over on the same ship, that "I would look into it." (I don't, I can't, and I realize why Larry never does. He tells someone else to. That's probably what I would do—all this went through my head—but just because I recognized the inevitability of this, I will look into it.) I asked Floyd. They were pulling a ship down to look at the seal. I heard myself order the parts (Floyd had said the seals were loose), check the drawings, call the engineer. Bart was going home early. I stayed. I don't know why. Then I went back to the ship. It was torn down. They had put a new nut and seal, the old one had no visible fault. I wanted to see why it leaked. I wanted to see it leak. "Run the ship up indoors without the rotor and we'll look at it." This was highly irregular but everyone responded. We got a pilot to run it. It had only run a minute when we saw the oil seeping up, *not* through the seal, but under the nut through the thread.

We had found it. Everyone recognized that we'd uncovered the mystery. As I went away, I said to myself: If you follow your own admonitions, you'll not rest there. See it through.

Sure enough, even after we'd put sealer on the thread, the leak persisted. Then we saw that it came through the keyway.

To get to this, it had to slip past the star washer. It was apparent the lugs on the star washer prevented the nut being drawn down tight. The oil got through under the nut into the keyway and out.

We put it together once more, leaving out the washer. It was OK.

Unwin said they'd torn twenty-seven ships down to change seals but this may have been an exaggeration.

The point is the incident made me feel good. I had proved myself again. The gloom that has been on me for days went away. The fact that I should be so influenced by a triumph of this sort made my higher self very disgusted with my gloating lower self. My higher self got really annoyed. All my practice and I get drunk on a few cocktails.

So my higher self is now really good and mad. I am going to forbid any more of this nonsense. This is what I call finding a trace of a path. I find that because of drinking this grape I cannot rise above what I want to rise above, therefore no more grapes.

March 6, 1947 (8:00 A.M.)

I should say that what I mean above is not just a repression of natural instincts. Rather it is a foregoing of apologies, of superstitions—a recognition of the law. I must be careful not to misinterpret it myself.

The zoo is my new book of philosophy. It is obvious that people are less fortunate than the animals—let's be careful now, lots of bromide puddles one might fall into.

But of our tendency to wear clothes . . . these extend beyond the body. Our minds too are clothed. Most of our life is spent dealing with the guise of our existence. It would be better to sit and glare at each other, or pick fleas, as entertain the pretense we are talking about the real.

Take love for instance. The Victorian clothing was to hide it in a trunk, packed with lavender and mothballs. The modern method is to parade it in a number of guises. "It is good for people to have a normal healthy attitude toward sex." Of course, this is putting the cart before the horse. It is impossible to have a "normal" attitude toward sex. "Normal" means average or mean. (An animal might be healthy by all ordinary standards.) Now sex is to a great extent one of the *ends* of our existence, as exploding is the end or purpose of a bomb. To reduce it to control or to a norm or mean, is to remove self-destruction from its realm. The female spider is said to devour the male at the completion of intercourse. But no self-respecting, which implies self-perpetuating, code would treat suicide as normal. [I have since read that male spiders have been observed to succeed in escaping from being eaten. So what is "normal"?]

We must be prepared to treat sex as if it extended beyond the confines of sane living, and if we don't we will simply not be talking about sex.

Our statement really reduces to: We can use discrimination about sex until it overcomes us.

But avoid one fallacy and another waits just around the corner. Suppose we have reversed our statement and say: Sex cannot be encompassed by the standards of normal living (which are servant to sex) (all's fair in love and war).

This also contains a fallacy, for it implies that the purpose of life is the preservation of species. This is highly dubious. Maybe the ultimate purpose is the attainment of self-realization, which will remove the need for the continual grinding of the projector that projects the cinema of life—or maybe this or maybe that— we could never know in the ordinary sense of knowing, on the grounds that a thing can't contain itself.

But we can know that sex energy has outlets other than procreation: art, creative activity, conquest, penetration, extension of the being of man.

Mind has the capacity to transcend all and any fixation, but to do so it must do work against natural forces. These natural forces are tendencies toward fixations. One of the most insidious of these fixations is concepts, conceptualizations. It is only the inventor who knows that there is no such thing as a helicopter because, having created it, he knows that what he has created is not it. But to everyone else, for no man can afford more than one chaos, a helicopter is a helicopter, a Jew is a Jew (referring to Sartre's *Portrait of the Anti-Semite*).

If Bell cancels all research, then the helicopter suffers a setback. Even assuming through the variety of enterprises being undertaken, a type finally emerges that is the answer, still there is reason to believe that this will be a slow, very slow process. There is no one at the present moment as well fitted as myself to devise this answer.

Now I have to decide. It is apparent to me now that Bell is not enough. There must be an even more radical and uncompromising approach to the problem than is made even in the variety of present-day attempts. I must decide between making that which was a means (*i.e.,* the helicopter) into the end, or continue on my initial course. Like a man going to California who stops to make a better bridge across the Mississippi—useful undertaking, possibly more worthy than the gold mine which was his first objective.

March 12, 1947

A remark I made to someone at Bell about my present attitude: "I'm just seeing what nature does when you let nature take its course."

Day at the plant. Beautiful day. Walked out over the airport to see one of the pilots make vertical auto-rotation landings [coming down vertically with the engine shut off—considered dangerous because without forward speed the rate of descent is much greater]. He discovered he could do this after reducing

velocity from 40 to 30, then to 20, and 10 miles per hour.
Finally he decided to try 0 airspeed, which still worked. This
indicates that the helicopter can be landed over a city on a
rooftop, or in a small parking area even if the engine fails. It
was a satisfaction to see the realization of this feature of the
helicopter at last, for I've always maintained it could be done
and it should be done. The rather conservative attitude of the
test pilots has prevented it.

A grim sense of the unreality of the possession of ideas.
"This was my idea," etc. The fact is the idea is going to come
through when the time is ready for it. It comes through you or
others. There is no final meaning in possession, nor is there in
nonpossession. We think that we have an idea. We are only
openings through which the unmanifest flows into the manifest.

Finally the gadget you sent for some time ago arrives through
the mail.

To Harriman I said, "Use the axe"—one of my favorite
expressions. With the axe we hack a path through the jungle. It
is a crude tool, but a carving tool, a pen knife, would tempt us
to do an unjustified degree of refined trimming. The axe makes a
relative path through the absolute. Twigs and small branches,
vines and grass, remain, but the caravan that follows tramps
them down in its progress.

March 13, 1947

Paid a visit to Mrs. Forman, back from Havana. She
gave me a Koan.

What the horse eats in California,
the ox digests in Maine.

Pardon my headlights but do I see a coaxial helicopter on the
compost heap? Or better—I see a bevel gear rusting on a
compost heap!

Not only dreams read the future. I am convinced that what is
happening is happening. Everything is everywhere. Coincidences
are misnamed. They happen according to law, but the laws, like
the universe, are vast. (Why did Mrs. Forman mention the Koan
that is so apt?)

The Crow's Nest:
    I am watching the chemicals boil. Now the color of the
solution is blue. Yesterday it was red. This is the very face
of illusion. Do not trust yourself. Who is the me who is
watching? Almost nothing, but he is all that will remain
when the stew has done with its cooking.
    So when I say these things, I send an observer aloft. He is
just a cabin boy and has no authority, but his position is
such that the grisly captain, and the tough first mate, will
accede to his warnings, for he sits in the crow's nest. What
are the surly crew muttering about below?

They say that a dog will return to his vomit. What vomit?
The sweet morsel you have vomited up. They say that the glue
is beginning to set, soon you will not be able to keep fussing
and adjusting the pieces. They say you cannot cut the end off a
piece of string. Someone asked what that meant. It means, said
another, that the abrupt and cruel end cannot be mollified.

March 20, 1947

The Bell situation again needs a new review. My last review concluded on the theme that Larry had a magic formula. By keeping away, he forced the people involved to assume and feel responsibility. But yesterday it seemed to me that the problem was too difficult to solve itself that way. This principle is true so far as the individual is concerned, *i.e.*, the inherent self-reliance, tone, and self-control of the citizen is fostered by an inefficient and unreliable government. I will go even further, and say the fabrications proceeding from individuals are also fostered and grow well in such soil. But insofar as the helicopter is itself a problem, *i.e.*, a problem of design, configuration, it will not profit by such abuse. This is the kind of objection that seemed to be sprouting yesterday.

In the first place, proceeding to specific instances, we found that production had decided not to change to the proper grease in the torque shaft bearings. Also, the system of making fixes was not working, for cases of improvements that were worse than the original condition keep arising. That basic bloodstream of new energy toward the design, so much needed now on certain items, especially the transmission, is cut off by the very structure of the organism which is Bell. The will to solidify is so much a part of the system, that only by reaction with the outside, and not by any internal mechanism, are new solutions found.

Take another specific example. The flight mechanic Carl Camp, the one person who really knows the mechanism, was confiding his troubles to me. The big shots were collected around the transmission, arguing about the gear track. Finally they asked him. He told them that all their judgments were based on a wrong assumption of the direction in which the gears were turning. Of course, telling them this invalidated their dubious conclusions. It made them mad. "It's a wonder I wasn't fired," he said. If management refuses to place someone in charge who is intelligent enough to understand what he is dealing with, or if it does not take sufficiently detailed interest to know that the need for such a person is critical, then is it not correct simply to say management is neglecting its function and the organism will suffer (instead of the more subtle argument that management by some higher rule allows these blemishes to exist)?

Of course, as with all rational arguments, we can point either way. What I really need is to get away from the situation, to see it in its true proportions.

I confess that reasoning alone can never solve the problem. How can we get any other criterion? Well, I can say this. Over a year ago I submitted a memo to Larry and later discussed with him in his office what I considered the only possible procedure. This discussion was precipitated by his statement to the press that he would make 500 helicopters in the first year. I said it would be foolish to make 500, make 50 or 100 and watch them carefully, learn the lessons and make the improvements—then go ahead and make more. He assured me that the 500 was only a device to satisfy the press, etc., that we would not make 500, and recognized the validity of my arguments. But I really don't think he has recognized my arguments.

To get back to the point. I said I would show another standard, independent of reason. Well, that's it. A year ago I had certain opinions, call them intuitive, but they differed in no way from my present opinions as to the course to be followed. What were these opinions founded on? Certainly not on the specific conflicts, confusions, and muddles we are now embroiled in. No, but they were founded on the confusions and muddles we *had been* embroiled in up to that time, and I knew that these muddles could not stop just because they were commanded to. I also know that the helicopter did not get where it was a year ago except by the highly coordinated activity of the group at Gardenville and assumed that the same rule should apply to its further development.

If this is correct, I'm wrong in shying away from the job of starting all over.

Toynbee, according to Bishop Pardu, has a lot to say about the significance of withdrawal. All the great men—Buddha, Mohammed, Christ—and many lesser figures—have withdrawn to return after a period with a grasp of higher forces within themselves, to return, Bishop Pardu emphasized, to take an active part in the world. This stirs me deeply. The instinct I have for withdrawal is justified by this. Or have I already withdrawn and lack the courage to go into action? I don't think so. Action comes without effort when its time is ripe.

March 22, 1947

Reactions to Dunne:

A disconcerting thing about the new phase of consciousness is that only under severe stress do its wheels start to turn. Now I feel normal (only a little sad). I am also mute. I dare not trust my ordinary thoughts. I sit waiting, a little ashamed of my distortions, but unable to change them. Or what I really mean is, if at the ball the charming lady places a slip of paper in our hand appointing a rendezvous for the morrow, how shall we continue the silly dance, go through the mincing minuet? If we see lurking in the shadows outside the masked visage of our executioner, how can we continue the casual conversation, sip the highball . . . or if you are sick of analogies, I will proceed directly to the point.

I am almost convinced that Dunne is right when he says that dreams are drawn as much from the future as from the past.

[This conclusion was so shattering I kept harping on it.] Don't worry if I happen to be saying the opposite of what I mean. You don't worry if somebody hands you your change with the coin showing tails. Turn it over, old fellow, you see I'm still creeping up on the quarry. Even as I circle, this young rabbit moves, so my course is like the path of the red dot on a tire.

So, if Dunne is correct, time is attention. Please give me the correct time. Either it is time for a theory or I better go to the bathroom. I am still Mr. Milquetoast Hamlet, and must make a play within the play, some more experiments to slow the show.

But really, don't you see the point? It is as though people were making bets on an issue that was already settled. *The New Yorker* had a story. . . . What are we sitting around for? The orchestra has left, the dance is over. . . . Or as though someone ran through the room saying the house is on fire, yet the ladies did not stop considering the choice of lace curtains, if, if . . . and yet that is not the point. That is Time 1, but there are other times, such as the time I met you or the time that goes sideways like our dreams, and if time the river overflows, it becomes a lake; a lake is only a river which hasn't found the way out.

So we go down, down, down, following the inevitable slope, acting as though we knew the where of our going, now and then turning, spreading out, seeking again the lowest point for our escape. Spread me as thin as butter on a cracker, still I seep out of my edges down, on down, to perdition and the sea. What did we see? We saw the sea.

A fire engine returns from a false alarm, and across the street an old man in a dressing gown looks out on Oakland Place through a table littered with knickknacks.

[The passage which began, "Don't worry if I happen to be saying" and ends with the fire engine, was one in which I was trying to express unconscious feelings. The next day I learned that the red helicopter, known as the "fire engine," had gone to rescue some fishermen but it was a false alarm.]

I see now in Hamlet much that I didn't see before. Through the veil of reality Hamlet pokes his sword of insanity. There are several theories of his insanity:

1. The oldest, that he was actually insane.
2. The second, that he was sane but feigned insanity.
3. The third, which I hereby announce, that he was superconscious in his insane utterances, that he was actually seeing through the illusion of the action sphere. "Have you a daughter, sire? Let her not walk in the sun, for the sun breeds maggots, etc."

There is that crow's-nest self that does not crave the new self.

I should have a debate between them. Then these pink opinions would show forth in their original bright coloring as red-and-white stripes.

To return to Hamlet. What is the ghost that he sees? The ghost is the glimpse of truth that stops him dead in his tracks, that knocks the values of his ordinary life off their ordered shelves and tables. The King becomes a murderer, the Queen an adulteress, action on the basis of his previous values has to stop, new acts must be devised. Thus Hamlet begins to see behind the screen. His habits of life have not prepared him to act on this new evidence; he sulks about, lashing out now and then with his insane jibes. Polonius is old enough and enough out of the "plane of conflict" to be able to afford recognition of some truth in Hamlet's utterances. The audience, however, not being in the plane of conflict can recognize the complete truth.

But the truth, the hard kernel of grit that has recently been inserted in my oyster self, still evades my grasp. There is that centrifugal force that throws everything out from the spinning center, making our statements tangent.

At least if one cannot pursue a truth by a well-aimed shot because of this centrifugal force, one can. . . .

The Crow's Nest:
    There is no solution on board the ship. The captain says one thing, the crew another, mutiny may or may not occur —to the crew the situation is intolerable. So my only salvation lies in what the cabin boy has to say. If he reports land in time there may be sufficient distraction to make all hands pull together.

I am greatly disappointed in my failure to learn my lessons. Months of stifling my vanity, my sense of injustice, instead of starving out these appendages, finds them still bursting with pressure, with the desire to trip me and send me reeling. The situation finds me far from calm, resigned; rather I'm bitter, sour, ready enough externally to act as though I'd reformed but still building up within—a kind of hard gallstone that may be worse than the poison that made it, because it is more solid, more insoluble. Too bad.

The only solution appears to be a parallel development of the higher self. It is beginning to attain more stature, perhaps even to walk; if it gets strong enough, perhaps it can cast off the other like an old shell.

Tomorrow I go to Washington.

March 23, 1947
(Washington, D.C.)

Reconsider and plan for resumption of Hatha Yoga. *Hatha Yoga* by Theos Bernard is the best I've found so far. It is more appealing, putting less emphasis on vague ideas like contemplation, more on the accomplishment of specific feats. The breathing was what especially impressed me last night.

The chapter headings:

1. *Asanas,* the postures. One of most important: Sirsasana. Headstand. Goal: 3 hours—took several months to reach 15 minutes. Generally on asanas, he says, assume posture, repeat 3–5 times. After a week hold 15 seconds. No special order. 1 to 1 1/2 hours on asanas.

2. *Purification.* This is emphasized. *Swallowing the bandage.* Three weeks to learn controlled vomiting—not long. *Basti* (colonic irrigation). Comes after Nauli. *Neti* (cleansing nasal passages). Draw water into nose and expel it through the mouth, etc. *Uddiyana* (exercise of stomach muscles). 5 rounds of 10 contractions (50) increased each week till 500, then a month of 500 per, then 750. Important that when mastered (1,500 contractions) it can be dropped. *Nauli* (after six months of Uddiyana). *Bhastrika* (bellows). Probably after Nauli.

3. *Pranayama.* Surprising thing to me now is emphasis on holding the breath. The technique was (after Bhastrika) 10 suspensions of 2 minutes each. I find a single suspension of 2 minutes difficult. (Did several 1 1/2 minutes last night.) He says

don't go beyond [stage of hearing] singing. He reached 4-minute suspensions after practice. Then (with tongue swallowing) reached 5-minute suspensions for 10 rounds. (This is already far in excess of anything I've heard of before.) He says: "Still this is far from the standard required by the tests for attaining the supernatural powers described in all Yoga literature. To acquire such powers it is necessary to hold the breath for an hour or more."

I asked the young prince how they could possibly drive 1,300 miles (yes, miles, not kilometers) a day for three days (the Ventimiglia auto race covers this distance in this time—from Turin to Regia, around Sicily, back to Regia and north again). He replied, "Oh, it's very simple. We drive 1,000 miles a day for a month for practice. Then it is not too hard to do the race." This was when I went to Italy in 1933.

The perspective this gives is interesting to me.

To myself 300 miles a day is enough. Four hundred would be a hard job, especially in Italy. To me the difference between 1,000 and 1,300 does not seem as great as the difference between 400 and 1,000, or 800 for that matter. But obviously this is not correct. A thousand miles a day can be achieved but 1,300 is difficult. This implies that my measuring, based on my own limit of 400 miles per day, is obstructing my conception of the problem.

I can recall often thinking, "This machine is rotating at 1,000 rpm. The noise is terrific. How can it possibly go any faster?" I would then increase its speed, the change in sound was what I expected, but it would still hold together. Similar misgivings attended each increase. My credulity was taxed, stretched, rather, until I could believe it could go further. Rather each step seemed to violate the sensible limit which some jury of good men and true, sitting in judgment in my mind, established as right and proper.

In fact, the progress of science has been doing almost continual violence to this sense of credulity. Take the fan on the helicopter. It operates at 4,500 rpm. It makes a terrific amount of noise and sets up an enormous blast of air. Now if someone came in and proposed to operate that fan, or one similar in size, at 10,000 rpm, the sense of reasonableness, the credulity of anyone who had experienced one would be upset. They might even deny the possibility. Yet the jet engine contains just such a device in its blower. About 500 horsepower going into a disk 15 inches in diameter.

If someone were trying to explain this to a conscientious audience of, say, 100 years ago, he would be faced with this adamant sense of incredulity. What would the intelligent reaction be to someone who announced something that exceeded credulity?

I think that the intelligent reaction would still start from the known. It would make careful check of the existing limits, seek to see why these limits existed, inquire as to the steps taken to overcome them, and demand to see, if not the actual, the abstract presentation of the actual.

A man from 1850 who has built a steam engine is, let us say, carried into the present and told about a 2,000 horsepower gasoline engine. His first reaction might be, oh, these fellows have some brand new thing we knew nothing about. But if he is really intelligent, he will say, the probabilities are they developed much further along the same lines that we were on. They probably did not depend on a new and startling discovery. He would therefore proceed to question thus:

What is the diameter of the pistons? How many? What is the piston speed? How is it fitted into the cylinder to overcome rubbing? How does the crank stand up against the forces imposed on it? (In merely asking these questions he would expand his picture, the possibilities of his own engine.) How do you machine the cylinders? (A very important question.) How can your gears carry such loads? How do you cut gears?

Just these last two questions alone would span tremendous profundities in the answering. He would experience almost as a revelation the method of cutting gears by generating, a process which automatically produces the exact curve required for smooth operation.

Having rationally and intelligently questioned the modern man, the nineteenth-century inventor would be compelled to say that there had been no break in the continuous perfection, specialization, concentration, that produced the new engine, just as there is no break from the root to the leaf in the tree.

He would then see that out of his own 10 horsepower

steam engine was produced one having 200 times as much power and no greater weight. Thus, the incredible would be developed out of what was at hand.

Over and over I have seen this. The art of magic is largely a matter of pushing things to their limits. Card tricks, etc., depend on taking advantage of many small effects, but principally depend on the development of techniques beyond the commonplace level, into the realm of the incredulous, but by continuousness.

March 28, 1947

We are now ready to take up this Yoga question again.

Mr. Bernard can, after let us say a year's training, hold his breath six minutes. This is already beyond credulity, if you know anything about holding your breath.

For myself, and also my brother, who beat the world's record for underwater swimming, three minutes is absolute tops. After this you go unconscious. He twice passed out while swimming under water.

But I find that I can believe that Bernard can do this when I recognize the fact of his practice, *i.e.,* he held his breath for 4 minutes 10 times in succession every day for an extended period. To do this there must have been a gradual adjustment of his nervous system to control the rate of metabolism. Otherwise, the body would use all its oxygen—he would suffocate. So, assuming this control, there appears to be no reason why it could not be extended to cover more than an hour, or perhaps months as in case of suspended animation (which certain animals can do anyway, so why do we doubt it at all?).

It is not so much doubt that is stimulating my argument.

Let us admit then that the Yoga practices lead to conscious

control of the nervous system, or rather that the conscious control of the breath forces the system to control itself. One way or another the art of suspending various chemical, psychological, etc., activities is gained. If, during this control, consciousness is retained, then it is but a step to freeing consciousness from the body, or is it?

March 29, 1947

Spent day at Camden Airport. Helicopters! On exhibit. Brantly coaxial. Kellet intermeshing. Autogiro. German Rotary Kite. Platt-Lepage, Herrick, Piaseki. Demonstrations by five Bell and three Sikorsky machines. Goodrich (Pat. examiner), Synesvelt. Bell personnel, Sikorsky, Bennett, Brie, Breguet, Brantly, Bradbury, Nickolsky, Sayre, Bigley. A great many people speaking to me. . . .

J. D. put on a terrific demonstration with Model 47.

I dreaded the next—a helicopter dinner at the Warwick. First was a meeting of "Twirly Birds," a club of helicopter pilots who had flown before VJ day. Choosing emblem. What is definition of having flown, etc.? Then the dinner.

After the awards came the speeches. Larry was toastmaster. "We'll have to stop experimenting and get those machines out where they can get to work." There's a lot in that. Maybe I shouldn't think any more about getting the helicopter better.

Why do I write about all this? Well, because across the pattern of smugness, the mutual back-scratching of these Helicopter Society-ites, I felt (and I am more aware of it now that it's over) another current which was genuine and had great power. People kept speaking to me with a sort of hope, people who were propelled by *want*, mostly the lone wolf inventors, not the white collar engineers, with their house of membership cards, their certifications of merit.

April 5, 1947

Looking closely at my fingers I could perceive an almost invisible refraction projecting from my fingertips. Against certain backgrounds it was possible to detect it. On the way to the library I elaborated on a plan. Go to Eastman Kodak, explain that I wanted a filter to photograph the human aura. I enjoyed seeing myself in this role. There would be two possible methods. 1. Filters (Dyacin). 2. Refraction: Place the fingertips in a beam of light which showed an enlarged pattern. With careful use of proper lenses, etc., the aura could be amplified. (Is it this aura that makes itself visible around one's shadow? Test would be whether an inanimate object makes the same aura.) Another plan would be to get in touch with Leopold Mannes who worked out Kodachrome—or to get the equipment oneself. Now that I've been through the Bell incident I can see Kodak's point of view. "We're busy. Just what do you want? So what?" and so on. It would require time, effort; you can't get other people to do your growing. Maybe all this is wrong. It's a yes or no test; not necessarily, but it would degenerate into one. After all, what one really wants is to see the aura, not to photograph it; one wants to know about it more than to see it—to get off the train to prove one's at Chicago precludes our going on to the coast. Now I think more of talking to Garrett [Eileen Garrett, a well-known sensitive and successful publisher, who later founded the Parapsychology Foundation]. Must meet her. You see how these projects are building up? Too many distractions. What is one doing but satisfying an urge to feel that one is doing something about it.

To justify my own acceptance of the paranormal I have: *Phenomena in my own life.* Rare but convincing. Football game.

[At a football game (which I didn't want to go to because football bores me) I was able to predict when touchdowns would be made.] Piano recital. Dunne effect. Helicopter (two instances). Meeting someone without appointment. Superconscious plans. Abstract poetry.

The Library of Congress Main Reading Room—an image: *I am a spermatozoa.* But first I am the male principle. I enter the building. A sign says "Readers only. Visitors keep out." It is necessary to lift the skirt. Here is the door. A sign says "Push." I push. Now I am in. A long-curtained corridor. Now I am a sperm. I crawl up and look for my egg. It is somewhere in the stacks, in the files. A conveyor belt will bring it to me. I will dive into it and lose myself forever in that warm and pulsing thing that without me is only inert, waiting.

That *ecstasy* of contemplation. It is the pleasure of pleasures. But it must also create itself. It must be worked out. The dream must somehow materialize. The helicopter was one that I managed to live through—eighteen years is a long time. Yet it is not the time that bothers me, but the fact that it's taken away, freezes before it's ripe. Or it dies before it's grown up. Next time the dream must be something that cannot be taken away. The statue that comes to life must not run off with the local swain. Whatever it is, *it must be made manifest.*

The fallacy of repetition as a scientific criterion of validity.
Maybe there is a fundamental restriction placed on truth by the requirement that it must be capable of repetition. Price says there is no single datum sufficient for scientific confirmation. Why does it have to be repeated? I have a forewarning of an event—it happens—this cannot be repeated. Suppose you required that to prove there was such a thing as a joke you must be able to repeat it. Obviously, it couldn't be repeated. Though I've heard people who seem to think so.

I have been wearing a blanket. I will continue to do so, but it may come about that I will throw it off.

Non-Yoga. I can squirt water on the ceiling—monkeys can do tricks.

April 8, 1947

Asked Robert [Morse] to make appointment with Mrs. Garrett.
Breathing unexplainedly successful.

April 9, 1947 (New York City)

Mrs. Garrett was with us in the Ritz Cocktail Lounge 2 1/2
hours and answered all my questions. Was extremely
interesting. Outstanding was her description of how she
controls the dice. First she puts herself into a state of
nondiscrimination, "where," she pointed to the knife on the
table, "this becomes indistinguishable from other objects—a
state of 'high carelessness'—then I roll this up and project it on
the dice. After two or three rolls they begin to come up with
my number. I act upon them while they are falling open to the
laws of chance. Then the curious thing is that they roll this
number after I've started to call another. Several rolls are
required before they change to the new number. Professor
Murphy is doing this with me. He wants me to work on the
growth of plants, to encourage some and not others."

Another time she took my new "Cado" pen which I'd bought
the day before and, holding it in one hand, proceeded to run her
other hand over it a few times. Then she started to describe
incidents that I recognized as having happened to me that

morning with Dave. She also described Dave—what he said to me and what I thought of him. I do not propose to make a case of this; it is not as remarkable as many authenticated by others, but it was noteworthy that she was able to do this in the crowded Green Room or whatever it was, where we were having tea.

She criticized Yoga, by which she meant contemplation. You can recognize them in the street, she said. But went on to say that she rolls on the floor, stretches, and takes breathing exercises morning and night. She enters into ordinary life just as much as anyone, takes her whiskey. I pointed out to her that what she did was Hatha Yoga. She asked me something about breathing. I said Dr. Williamson showed me how. She repeated this remark as though it were significant, but whether for or against I couldn't say for sure, although the context would imply for.

After this we sat for an hour recovering. Then wandered out to dinner at Caviar. We couldn't find it so we went back to look it up in the telephone book, then went toward 49th St. Someone hailed us. It was Roy Little, who sat with us at dinner. [Roy Little, founder of Textron, later (1952) bought Bell.] Because of his interest in the helicopter I asked him his opinion of Stettinius [the financier who had been trying to take over Bell]. He said, "That's funny, I've just had dinner with him!" He'd find out more and let me know, but this was not all. For some time Priscilla and I had talked about going to Nassau. Roy was going to join his wife there on the 26th. Would we come? (I had made a tentative date for the 25th in New York, anticipating this trip.) So the 26th would be OK.

April 12, 1947

I must note more fully the other incidents which occurred in New York.

Dr. Williamson, after patiently correcting a number of exercises I'd been doing, and giving me more, one to cause relaxation and others to straighten my back (the Bow, the Cobra, and lying on the bed with head hung over), then got to breathing. I was to take the seated position with legs crossed, breathe out slowly, at the same time bending forward till my head touched the floor. Then inhale slowly, letting the air lift me till I was sitting up straight. Exhale through mouth, inhale through nose. Repeat this 20 times (counting back and forth on 10 fingers). Then hold the breath, and concentrate on the singing one can hear in one's head. "Think of yourself flying on a radio beam," on a narrow "razor's edge." Then after about a minute use the fingers to hold the nostrils. As you begin to crave air let your body go, let it thrash around like a bronco but ride it in a relaxed manner. Let your stomach pump in and out (as it did when you were in the womb and it obtained nourishment from the umbilical cord).

I did this and held my breath for what I thought to be 3 minutes (180 counts) which he timed as 2 1/4 minutes, which was all I could stand, or thought I could stand. (In a previous first attempt I did not hold my nostrils and believe that I was drawing in air all the time.) He instructed me to do this three times, not holding the breath more than 3 minutes (some of his students were holding for 11 minutes, "blue boys").

That evening, about midnight, after several stingers, I did my regular 200 contractions, plus 3-minute headstand, and followed with the breathing. The first round was without special comment, rather poor. The second round felt good from the start. As I held my breath beyond 120 counts violent trembling set in. I think I reached 180 counts when an extraordinary feeling of elation and lightness set in accompanied by an intensity of consciousness of nothing. This was not an especially gratifying sensation, like drinking water when thirsty or coition or the like, but it was nevertheless a supersensation, which I would go far to experience again. It had some of that ultimate satisfaction that one reads about, the superconscious elation, etc. I would describe it as becoming the ring of a bell. In addition, I felt tall and straight. The third round gave me almost the same sensation again and I slipped into bed feeling like a rod of glass filled with ice water. I was not conscious of any thoughts but I was conscious of being a thing—empty and clear. I do not believe this is what is described as the serpent power, nor any form of enlightenment especially, but it was a sensation beyond any that has occurred to me before.

I did not go to sleep for some time. I lay in bed feeling this icicle feeling with an unbounded joy. After I fell asleep, Priscilla woke with the hallucination of seeing a man at the door or something.

The next morning the exercises did not have this effect. I may say that holding the breath till this trembling occurs requires about all my willpower. It seems one is inviting death.

That night I did only 2 rounds (it was late). After the trembling came a period of calm. My body quieted down completely.

The next morning I did the breathing in the bedroom. (The flushing of toilets in the hotel made such a reverberation in the bathroom as to distract concentration.) This time just the trembling, then the calm, and then came a violent jumping up and down. My body jumped up and down like a frog. I was scared to go on.

Williamson expressed no surprise at the symptoms over the phone. He said to do only one set of 3 rounds a day until I got used to it. On the train I could not do the practice. Last night I had a bathroom scale I had brought from the plant and weighed myself during and after the suspension but there was no perceptible change of weight. I seemed to suffer more pain in holding to 3 minutes (actually a count of 180) and go through the trembling (which is sometimes not all over my body, only my arm, etc.) rather quickly. The calm was not too clear-cut, then some jumping, but not the same mental elation as before, especially nothing that lasted after the suspension.

As I write this, and often today, I've noticed the singing in my head, which is apparently the aim.

Went to the zoo with C. today. I realized how the monkeys belong in this phase that I am in. They show one how to live naturally to some extent. Also I feel a growing sense of painting with my muscles.

Breathing exercises last night were promising on the first round, less so on the second and a little better on the third. The last time my suspension was for about 200 seconds. I found by using the clock that my seconds are if anything a trifle long, *i.e.,* I count about 55 to a minute. On one round, I forget which but I think it was the first, the hopping up and down was sufficient to lift me several inches off the floor. I doubt if I could do this consciously.

There is some resemblance to ground resonance in the helicopter. First, we have lateral resonance (trembling) then a period of calm, then longitudinal resonance. The difference is that the trembling is of higher frequency than the jumping up and down.

The fact that Patanjali [Hindu philosopher, author of Yoga Sutras] states that the sequence ends with walking on air made me want to weigh myself. However, the result was negative. I almost said the result was, of course, negative. The fact that I go so far as to weigh myself is the interesting part. The negative result means nothing, any more than not finding a buried treasure means there is none. If there were to be a positive result I would not be ready for it anyway. Considered physically alone, my body is not ready for these higher practices. During the final suspension I could well see the reason for the cleansings insisted on by the Yogis. My bowels created some gas and might have thrown off some waste matter, so violent were the contortions.

I think I can detect a difference in the degree of painfulness obtained by concentration on the singing. It is hard to concentrate, of course, but concentration appears to relieve the situation slightly. I also notice that sitting up straight with my hand on the nostrils seems to delay the beginning of the need for air. At first, for a minute, sometimes one and one-half minutes, there is no discomfort whatever; in fact, it is a highly invigorated feeling.

My morning exercise is now 200 contractions. I find I can do only 5 rounds of 20 comfortably, then 10 rounds of 10. A 4-minute headstand is about my limit. It's easy enough to stay up longer but when I get down my back is painful. My arms are somewhat painful now. I did ten 50-second suspensions (à la Bernard continuously) to fill in, since Williamson said to do his 3-minute suspensions only once a day. I've dropped most of the asanas except the Bow and the Cobra.

This morning I felt rather sleepy—uncomfortable. The singing seems to grow louder.

April 15, 1947

Hatha: Pain in the arms returned—Sunday night very tired (no reason) but managed to do 2 rounds. Had difficulty holding 3 minutes. A sort of deep humiliation comes over me in this, as I see the utter powerlessness to master physical limitations. After the pain of holding the breath 3 minutes the fear of God is driven into one in an emotional way. One gasps for air. The torture has stopped; one grovels, sobbing like a child who has lost a race.

Tired again Monday (yesterday). Did 2 rounds in A.M.—not much better. Monday night, however, both rounds—especially the second—were easy: 3 1/2 minutes was as far as I went, and I might have gone further, but the interesting thing was that the painful character had abated. Up to 2 minutes no disagreeable sensation whatever. Then some discomfort. Then as the body started to gallop (like a horse) I felt very little discomfort. In all these recent efforts the violence of trembling and jumping is much reduced. It appears that the body is becoming adjusted, although it may just be a variation that will start the other way. One trouble with the night sessions is that it is hard to go to sleep afterward.

Standing on head 4 minutes is fairly easy now. 300 contractions is not hard, though I rest every 100. Still can't keep up at the rate of 20 per suspension, have to intersperse a few 10s.

Of course there is such a thing as false information. *Time* had an article on the Hoppicopter, *Life* one on Hiller [Stan Hiller, of California, one of the other early helicopter designers]. I know these articles are false because I know the people and I know what they are doing. This is very often the case. But it does not invalidate the existence of the marvelous. Even if all the things I've been told about—Cayce—Cummins—Osty—Fort—Yogis—Buddha—Christ—are omitted, I have seen a few with my own eyes—prophetic dreams—seeing at a distance. And I can make people turn in a restaurant. So the existence of false information does not dispel the occurrence of the impossible.

Then there is that "W" pattern again. That which is reputed false is true. That which is reputed true is false. We should get serious about what's funny; we should laugh at what's serious. Why?

We should be more serious about life, but didn't Mrs. Garrett say the state of "high carelessness" was necessary to supernormal activity? Are these things inconsistent? No. For when we say we should be more serious, we mean serious about that which normally we slough off. And when we say "high carelessness" we mean that which we normally hold sacred.

(Reading over the above, it doesn't satisfy.)

My state of mind, or state of being is now such that I'm not bothered by thoughts. I seem to be quivering, in a state of ache; it is not comfortable or uncomfortable. My body is highly sensitized, yet it is not puking anything up. I can sit long periods with no thought—not absolutely no thoughts, but thoughts are thinning out, strays wander by, the road is not crowded with traffic as it used to be.

This quivering state (am I a Quaker?) is anticipatory and frightened (not mentally, it corresponds to the physical state of being frightened). It is perhaps consciousness per se since I find myself not wanting to do anything. It was helpful at the concert; I felt like a spare violin, reverberating (physically again) to the sound waves. This sensation was not in my ears, it was in my legs. But it does not appear to have any value elsewhere, although it helps me to hold a certain reserve. Yesterday at lunch I had less trouble than usual not talking. In fact, talking is more awkward than ever. One is surprised to find oneself launching a few sentences.

Now to correct the non sequitur of the sentence above— writing falls short of the goal. My state of mind is nonverbal. Why bother to write? For the following reason. The books I brought back from New York represent a span of years in the consciousness of psychic phenomena. Gurney, Myers, and Podmore, in 1886. Richet in 1923. Cummins in 1946. It is apparent that this consciousness is growing. The depth of focus changes. The early writers seem to have a much shallower view of the extent of the marvelous. It exists for them as a narrow and special phenomenon. With Richet it broadens and goes further. With recent books it gets much more general, more unbelievable, more significant. What has enlarged is consciousness (of the marvelous). Presumably the phenomena themselves have not changed. But the moral is that, regardless of the limitations of consciousness and of words, they *are* what we have to deal with. Even though reality is behind this screen of illusion, we cannot trust "nonverbal" methods. This is also borne out by the poor showing made by Yogananda, *Autobiography of a Yogi.* So we have to keep on struggling to build something out of words, even though words are not it.

Interesting Experiment:
I have been reading most of the day. Furze Moorish last. I went to sleep with the book open in my lap, my knees up, my feet on the couch. I experienced difficulty in waking up but finally got my eyes open.

However, I was still asleep. I tried with all my might to draw my hands apart but they would not budge. If I closed my eyes they would seem to come apart but I could see through my eyes that they did not move. I could even feel the skin stretch as my "will" pulled on my arms trying to move them. But they would not. Then with my fingers I made the pages fan. I was convinced I was doing this until again I looked through my eyes and saw my hands absolutely motionless on the opened book. I looked at the top of the book where I seemed to be flipping the pages. My hands were not there, nor were they at the lower edge. I was dreaming the sensation of thumbing the pages while I looked at my hands asleep.

I could go more to sleep or wake up more but was interested in teetering on this middle phase. After I woke the angle of vision seemed to increase, though not the clarity. I wished I had tried to read. (When I woke I noticed the angle of vision included the windows which were visible above the edge of the book—in sleep the edge of the book appeared to be the limit of the visual field. I did not try to move my eyes.)

Shakespeare has Lady Macbeth walking in her sleep, moving her hands, etc. "Her eyes are open," says the nurse. "Aye, but their sense is *shut*," says the doctor, which is something else. My case was the opposite, for my eyes alone were not asleep.

This is not entirely new to me. I think I've had very short intervals when I waked unevenly, etc., but this time it was very pronounced and protracted. So I might suspect it was due to Yoga practice. If so, it poses the question of the advisability of this activity.

Furze Moorish says Hatha Yoga is dangerous for Westerners, may cause insanity, etc. My painful arms and shoulders are somehow a result. Should I not ask myself whether I could not just as easily do some harm to my mind with this practice?

The answer must be that I am drawn by the indication that supernormal manifestations do exist. Their existence puts scientific, common sense, rational interpretation of life into the scrap heap. We are faced with a new mystery. Or, what is even more significant, the materialistic drapes that seemed to explain the phenomena of life have gotten torn and disclose a new texture altogether. It is as though an old master started to peel, revealing another picture beneath it. We realize that it is not genuine; we are curious to find what's beneath. What I wish to convey by this image is that the materialist explanation can no longer get by on the excuse that it is an "aspect" of reality. For it is invaded in its own realm.

So the issue is very serious. So much so that one can afford to change one's course. I had planned to study mind (the helicopter was a temporary excursion into the realm of the objectively provable, a guinea pig, etc.), but now that I'm in it I find the initial assumptions have to be swept aside. There may be no meaning in the implications of my title, "Mechanics of Mind." I would not now so entitle it. Mind appears to be the all. Hence transcends "mechanics."

At plant yesterday. My attitude was an almost psychopathic dread coupled with boredom. I decided to face it and visited different departments. The appearance of everything going well was supported. The old troubles were gradually being corrected, new ones were appearing at a declining rate. Certain key people were "seeing the light." The helicopters in the field were garnering fresh honors and making few mistakes.

I found it was difficult or impossible to inject myself in any useful way (except perhaps morale). By this I mean, of course, that the ice has formed and it is no longer possible to swim. The need for and the means for basic molding is gone. This is a comprehensive statement, for by means is implied the complete metamorphosis of the means of making helicopters.

Now this brings me to a general evaluation. My judgment has been too conservative. I don't mean I was wrong, for the method I would have used would have been sure to work. But the other method is also working. What is wrong with my evaluation? The most grievous error is the possibility of not having confidence in processes exterior to myself. "Never understimate the power of a woman," "Don't sell America short" are other instances of this error. I have been conscious of this possibility and have tried to take it into account.

Another error is that my method, which would place a premium on intelligence, has the objection that it would end up with people that were too intelligent for their jobs and would tend to get out of step. The other gradually brings the people up, "educates them to their jobs," at the same time that the job tends to get easier (the design gradually gets more or less foolproof). This ends with the job taxing the individual enough to keep him interested; at no time is there that demoralizing overtaking of the job.

There Is a River [book about Edgar Cayce by Thomas Sugrue]

What mental adjustment can we make to the recital of facts here—deny all? Accept with reservations? What I want to say is that there is evidence the author dressed up his story, a little unevenly since in the first part of the book we started to think of Cayce as a sensitive lad who was inspired. In the middle, it is told as though Cayce was a very humdrum dope, having only a certain moral fortitude, in fact a completely dual personality from the sage who hands out learned diagnoses. This weakness of the author we admit; in fact, we must allow it in any storyteller. But its admission in no way affects the unexplainable miracles paraded. The true story might be less dramatic; it might be more dramatic—the miracle is there. Not only does it wipe out the impressiveness of the American Medical Association, it shatters the whole fabric of modern civilized life.

What is our scientific civilization? Nothing? No, it is a very impressive something, but this something is really not what we thought it was. What it is, is the power of duplication. Once upon a time there was magic. Civilization learned to reproduce, reduce to formula, and duplicate a part of this magic. That is our world of science. The rest of the magic has been tossed on the junk heap. We are now scratching around trying to piece it together again.

Science, therefore, as such, is very wonderful, very impressive. But it is not a means of knowing truth. Not by any means. This is apparent when we make a careful examination of the history of science. Or the history of invention. Or, if we conscientiously seek out the final answers on, say, physics, it will be found that there is no evidence that denies unduplicatable magic.

It is the tangent to science that is opposite to the ancient mysteries. Scratch the paint and you find blood. Blood everywhere—people who swallowed test tubes of germs— predictions that failed—a procession of irreconcilables that only the slop-slop of the insensitive house painter, indifferent because unaware, can have the gall to cover up.

April 23, 1947

This A.M. and yesterday A.M. did 4-minute suspensions without much discomfort. Considerably less hopping and trembling. Can reduce these to zero by "swooning" (letting the will drop, imagining one is completely without support).

May 11, 1947

Helicopter crash in Seattle killed pilot and CAA instructor. I heard this on my visit to Bendix Helicopter Thursday. This time I was not so completely upset as last year. . . .

When I got to Bendix the girl said they had been trying to reach me by phone from Bell. It was the Seattle crash. Bart had gone out. Nobody knew much about it. The wreckage lay at the bottom of the lake. . . .

[Since I could not learn more about the wreck until I returned to Buffalo, my notes continue with the news at Bendix.]

I was told the company [Bendix Helicopter] was out of funds —down now to $150,000. The helicopters had a total of sixty hours. What was left was a good group, which had made good progress. The new configuration with see-saw rotors was about the same we have at Bell. The pilot used to work at Bell, got a lot of dope from us. O. had consulted after he left. I felt obligated to tell about the magnitude of side-wind force so they won't kill themselves, but they had already had some bad scares.

In one way there was not much to the Bendix helicopter. It had nothing new. It wasn't as far along as they seemed to think. There were probably some major factors to be recognized aside from the innumerable items prior to production. In another way it was remarkable that they had gone through what they had, Gardenville fashion, and made helicopters that flew. There was no central brain power either. It shows that there was nothing unique about Gardenville except that we did it first.

On the train back to New York I sat with the assistant treasurer at Bendix. He told me something of the financial problems—which, simply stated, are: no money and little prospect with the market for aviation so soft. They hoped to get by on short-term loans. Naturally they can't make it with the machine, as far as it is now from actual production.

As we parted I told him my plan of long ago—to take the initial capital and invest it in AT&T and live on the income. If anyone kicked, just give him back his money. It looks as though the problem is not a stable helicopter, but a stable financial basis.

One might go to the insurance companies (who have money to invest) and point out the problem. There is a lot of money around. The stockholder method won't work because you can't personally explain the situation to a whole lot of hysterical owners. What we need is a new concept of financing.

The very desire for a long shot, which is the basis of venture capital, is the ruination of the ventures, for when the going gets difficult the prospects become gloomy and the money is withdrawn or is not forthcoming. So we should have a "stabilizer bar," a control base that was not influenced by prospects.

Is it possible to change the self?

I feel that this is happening to me. Since there is no self nature in persons, this is theoretically possible. I used not to want to lose my individuality, but now I would like to. The Hindus are unanimous in asserting that the ultimate self has no properties; it is an ultimate essence that cannot be characterized.

One asks, if the ultimate self is without form, why does it live through many lives, how is it modified by its successive lives?

May 14, 1947

Last night Bart and Tom came after supper. We discussed
matters at Bell and resolved to start our own company. Matters
have been coming to a head recently with another attempt of
management to bypass the original helicopter group. The
accident in Seattle is not being faced honestly and the result on
Floyd has been to make him serve notice that he will no longer
remain on contract. Similar dissatisfaction is general. The
chance of the company operating on management's theories is
slim.

In the past my reaction has been a mixture of wanting to get
on to other fields (philosophy) and discouragement with the way
things were turning out. I still believe in my original plan of
going into other than mechanical study at this stage. But I find I
cannot walk out on the helicopter. While I can lose interest in it
as a science with no difficulty, as a human problem it remains a
problem. As time goes by it seems more and more apparent that
a mess will develop. Not only will we not sell enough machines
to support the present company, but the soil will be so polluted
by the bad reputation of the helicopter that it may never recover.

Philosophically I am willing to face any result. In a way I
would be glad to see it vanish from the face of the earth. But
death is ugly and life tenacious. The corpse does not expire until
it is hacked beyond recognition and pools of blood lie about. I
am willing to face the music, if it be punishment for having
brought fire from Olympus—let the kites claw at my entrails. I
had even hoped, by not taking credit, not to receive the blame,
but the screen is not impervious.

So it comes to this, that even after renunciation of the
rewards of activity, renunciation of power and ambition,
someone is being hacked to pieces in the next room and one

cannot concentrate on the philosophical studies.

I am therefore faced with the alternative of going down with a bad situation, or lending my help to Bart, Tom, and as many others as may be needed, for there are more than enough, to try to steer a stable course. At worst it can be no worse than what now exists. At best it can be not only a solution to the helicopter but an experiment of a much higher plane—a conscientious experiment in economics, which the world needs more than gadgets.

At various times I've felt the need of a school. However, I can find no students. I would have to hire one to listen, like Pythagoras. But the school is an absolute necessity for the stable development of principles (ideas). Two reasons support the last statement. One is my brother Brinton's reason, which he got from Gurdjieff, that a teacher is necessary; the other, that I have found two heads are better than one if geared to the same problem. Last night I felt moved by the loyalty of Bart and Tom, and moved by their fundamental agreement on issues which we are emotionally one on, not because of what can be reasoned, but because of a deep conviction that has resulted from living through the thing together. On top of this I was concerned at a vista of frozen standards, and of rigidities of design. Bart was all for Floyd, whose merit I recognize, but whose Swedish stubbornness and lack of enthusiasm for departures has been a trial for me. But beyond all this I saw a deeper vista, a vision that hushed my even commenting on it, of us all as tools of an experiment, one of which maybe we didn't even know the shape. Philosophy is still my goal; maybe it must be worked out through these earnest people. They are not free enough to be earnest about principles of life, but they are high-minded enough to be earnest about the helicopter. The helicopter is part of the whole and therefore is the whole— which led me to say last night that this time I was metaphorically catching the bull by the tail, by which I mean that same concession that Buddha made when he drank the goat's milk offered him.

If this be false rationalizing, I hope I can find the weakness. Or if I may judge by previous experience, let it be false, the currents lie too deep for geodetic discovery.

May 16, 1947

Day before yesterday another helicopter crash in Providence.
Two killed. Half an hour later Dave, Floyd, D., O., and myself
were flying to Providence. We knew nothing about what had
happened. Someone said the torque shaft flew into the rotor. As
I thought about it, I remembered what I'd written that morning
about Prometheus having his entrails eaten by vultures and was
annoyed at the melodramatics. The hound of heaven was
pursuing me. Had I not surrendered to the hound, had I not
said, "I give up. What should I do?" Then I realized that the
God who is to say what you should do is not some outside
authority. The answer must be from the self. Well, if the self is
the world mind or a part, then the "me" is only its vehicle, and
I, my inner self, must not identify myself with the painful
experiences of the vehicle.

At the crash we examined the wreckage. The explanation
came to me very soon. The pillow blocks had failed, making the
rotor entirely out of control, so that it struck the tail during
flight and as it hit again and again, broke the machine as it
descended. No one had any other explanation. My feeling
became independent of misery. I was stage director of a tragedy.
That night after dinner with the operator of New England
Helicopter, who was a very nice boy, and after telephone
messages to all the officials of Bell, telling them we must ground
the ships, which Dave and I insisted on, I talked to Larry, who
was in Virginia with the head of the Civil Aeronautics Agency.
Then to CAA and Service, instructing that telegrams be sent.

The next morning we were all out again looking at the wreck
and searching the lower end of the airport, the woods, and the
swamp for evidence. An important piece of the wreck was
one-half of the stabilizer bar which was presumably in the

swamp. We had boots but they were not long enough so I
rolled my pants up to my crotch and waded around. The water
was cold, the day warm. Fresh green grass was coming up
among the dried yellow mat of the year before, the ferns were
just beginning to uncoil—the redwing blackbird squawked his
protest. I plunged into the cold stream on what looked like a
clean sand bottom and sunk up to my hips. All through the
swamp were clusters of bramble bushes and to prevent sinking
in further these had to be grabbed. It was tough going, but
there was magic in the place and the day. Dave flipped a
12-inch perch out of the stream. The bar was not found.

Others agreed that the pillow blocks had failed early in the
chain of events, and this was confirmed by finding a micarta
washer on the road very near where the accident must have
started.

Everyone was infected with the wild spell of the swamp and
at lunch we talked about hermits. The airplane pilot recounted
how his pal had been lost for months in the jungles of Burma,
had to eat raw monkey, and was finally found wandering
delirious, his weight down to 85 pounds from 190.

After lunch we had the CAA hearing. It was simple enough.
No one volunteered anything; they seemed to expect me to
explain and make decisions. I outlined the conclusions I had
come to as to what had happened. First, the pillow blocks failed,
so that the rotor was loose on the mast. The engine wound up
the controls, twisting them above the bar. The rotor, now
entirely out of control, struck the tail boom over and over again,
gradually demolishing it. Pieces of tail boom and blades were
scattered as the machine came down. Finally, the rotor dropped
into the path of the bar and the bar struck the trailing edge of a
blade. This smashed the bar, which flew off into the swamp,
pulling the lower control rods out through the Houdaille units.

There was no evidence to dispute this account and no other
suggestions, so it was accepted. I asked to take what was left of
the pillow blocks and the bar back to Buffalo, which was
permitted. Of course, I explained that if we could not prove that
the pillow blocks were bad forgings, or weak in some way, or
couldn't find some force large enough to break them, we would
be in a real mystery. We got in the Beechcraft and were back at
the plant by 6:30.

When I got home I called Bart who had already begun on a program to prove the pillow blocks weak, etc.

The next day Bart and I went up to see Floyd. He and the rest of the pilots were scattered around the pilots' room, their feet on the desks, casually discussing possible causes of the wreck. Here the opposite atmosphere prevailed. As each idea was brought up, it would be weighed, discussed for inconsistencies, and rejected. Now and then other points came up for discussion. An interesting one was stability of the cabin ship. It was almost unanimous that the original bubble model without tail covering was a much better configuration from the point of view of safe flying. (The cabin model is unstable—it has to have a stabilizing fin on the tail. This gets in the down draft or out of it at certain speeds, making curious things happen. The ship rears up on its nose, etc.)

The discussion broke up. I heard H. talking about the bubble. I went over and asked him more. He was talking about the radio and glove compartment of the cabin obscuring vision in auto-rotation. He also said people who get rides always comment on the visibility from the bubble, not so from the cabin. Had he noticed the difference in noise? Yes, he had—and he liked being able to look back as he can do in the bubble. Since this was one of the old arguments with management, I was pleased to hear the truth was coming out. [The cabin model was withdrawn only after customers insisted on the bubble.]

Making another helicopter company in Buffalo does not ring true. I find myself thinking about going to India for this purpose. This "rings" truer.

May 24, 1947

Factory manager fired yesterday.

I am now gaining confidence. I am ready to condemn the Bell philosophy as unsound because atheistic. Larry says no man is indispensable.

But the Bell organization is a dead thing without the central life principle that makes an organism, even a business organization, a going concern. It is this central core of vitality that erects the specialized system which is the externally visible "body" of the organization. It is this very "life principle" that makes it true "that no man is indispensable."

This being true, the present cacophony of tragedy (firing the factory manager, cutting production) is not a reform. It is a blundering reflex.

May 27, 1947

Last night the Budapest String Quartet. I was reluctant to take the time, but decided I could think. So I made a special effort to concentrate on the Koan Mrs. Forman gave me several months ago.

> The horse eats hay in California. The
> ox digests it in Maine.

This now seems to state the very problem of Bell, so its solution would solve the latter. My thinking pursued the following course:

The horse is Bell. They eat. The ox is us. We digest. The food creates a reaction on us which we are unable to transmit to the horse. Perhaps the hay is poison, but we are unable to warn the horse. A third element, a link, is necessary to connect us to transmit our digested knowledge. More generally, it is the problem of two bodies. Referring now to Boehme, the incidence of the 1 on the 2 (force reacting on matter, etc.) creates a struggle. The struggle continues until it can be resolved into a harmony. Or the question may be considered in time. Normally one would say the horse eats the hay, the ox digests the same hay. But the problem as presented conveys the idea of simultaneity; *i.e.,* the horse is eating, the ox digesting, so that the ox is digesting hay the horse ate previously. So if a signal returns from ox to horse making a statement about the hay, there is a lag. The statement applies only to the hay the horse ate a while before. So we have dynamic instability. The horse is always eating new hay to which the information conveyed by the ox is not applicable. So we may think of the horse as a next generation, which the older generation is tempted to advise. Hence we come to the conclusion that the horse is being reborn continually and ignores his past actions. So for an answer to the Koan we chose an image which conveys the idea of perpetual renewal.

> Dawn breaks with no thought of the
> yesterday that was clouded.

Such a solution implies that, for all our forebodings, others will pick up the helicopter and carry on, ignoring our forebodings. That does not mean we must retract our forebodings or that Bell is right. It means we are both wrong.

Mrs. Forman says there are unique answers to these Koans. If so, and I still don't have the answer, then more profundities will come up.

Thursday

Since we had not been able to find the cause of the Providence wreck, I had decided to take a piece of the helicopter blade to Eileen Garrett to have her "psychometrize" it. Called Eileen Garrett about an appointment made the day before and was told to come right over. Then my spirits picked up. The air had cleared enough to see the smartly dressed and pretty women on the street. Eileen got to work immediately and took the piece of rotor blade, felt it, looked at nothing in particular, then started to talk about a larger machine. Was that it? No. That must have crept in since I carried it about with me. Then more about the small machine. The pilot was "unstable, had recently tried to enter the church, had twice before had trouble with the machine, was outwardly gay, careless in fact, but not stable. He was also not its master. The machine had a lightness about it. It was a good one. Then there were ripples. No, not in the air, in metal." She started to talk about metal flowing like butter, drew a diagram, egg shape, indicating little streaks. I said pillow blocks were examined by Aluminum Company, were declared sound. Then I drew pillow blocks. The end view aroused no response; the side view did. Eileen pointed to the position of the break. "Yes, there." When I drew the static stop, she said, "Yes, it's cradle-shaped. You will have to work on that. You will add something here," and drew rounded pads on the ends.

[It was over a year later, visiting the Providence operation, when I was told that the pilot of the wrecked helicopter had been having a nervous breakdown at the time of the accident and was about to enter a monastery.]

June 10, 1947

Situation at Bell worse, if that is possible. Impossible to get our team together. . . .

Now to return to the world within the world. I am thinking now that what's wrong in the helicopter picture is that we have not been able to present clearly our need for working the way we have to. Attempts to start our own company will only postpone the true issue, which is the clear setting down in a way that can be understood by all, or at least management, just why we have to work through the individual instead of through the system.

So far so good, but the answer is that it will not be recognized or understood until experienced (by management or the opposition). This implies waiting until it is so understood, which is what we've been trying to do but with no visible progress. Why? Because "the experience" is too indirect. A job is messed up because of just what I'm speaking of, but it is blamed on almost everything else. The person in charge is fired and everything starts over again. The one who has learned most is pushed aside.

I find myself persistently trying to do what all the esotericists say cannot be done, give logical expression to truths that they say can only be experienced. Even this I had recognized before, though, and so one more step and I'll be there.

There must be some personal bias on my part in the direction of expecting that the stupid ones must be cajoled into partaking of higher knowledge. This explains why I want to explain. It looks like a bad trait, and it carries with it the implication that I'm not sure of my ground, which lack of confidence leads to my effort to persuade others. (It is a general rule that if "the lady protests innocence too much, she is guilty.")

If, on the other hand, I behaved in a more temperamental manner, and just acted mysterious, I would be accorded natural respect, the last remnant of that tribal superstition which conceded special authority to medicine men and priests.

It now occurs to me that this is happening all over the world over and over again. The same weakness may even now be betraying many companies. What then? Why, they will fail—and the world will wait for a species to arise that will not harbor this congenital weakness.

The thing we call Gardenville is becoming and would become a sort of hallowed tradition to its vigorous youth. Yet each step in its growth is a step in the direction of the freezing of function. If I really respect what was Gardenville, I must throw it away. As long as we have expert machinists, we will make expensive masts for the coaxial. What started as pieces of tubing, became, because we had such expert mechanics, highly accurate hollow shafts, straight and concentric, ID and OD [inside and outside dimensions], within a few thousandths.

I dreamed about a simple machine—an engine, an automobile transmission, two pieces of tubing, a seat, all fastened to a sled of 2×8s—rigged up with the utter simplicity that a man on a desert island uses to make a raft.

The king is dead, long live the king. Now I could see that all appurtenances are the paraphernalia of death, and that death is the removal of appurtenances. Each wave must rise and fall, until that one comes whose rising comes at just the right moment and place to trip the trigger that sets in motion the next action. Larry was making a mistake, to be sure, putting his all on the wave that was already collapsing. But I, letting Gardenville slip into oblivion, was avoiding one, for both waves would be too soon.

Tuesday (Buffalo)

Kafka set my brain young again. This feeling of fear—it seemed to become suddenly important. I felt it so often. Would the conductor accept my ticket? What was *The Castle* for me? I thought of the Bell plant and the helicopters flying over it. Wasn't there with me that dread that it would not permit me to enter? Wasn't it present in my every encounter? It was not quite the Kafka fear; I am more afraid of the unknown than authority. But the terrifying waiting for the letter to come, the fear of the system? What system? The Bell helicopter that was my own child, now something that appalls me. A king who was afraid to walk out of his own castle lest he not be allowed to return. . . .

Is it conceit, or insanity, or insight that makes me see all reality arranging itself into a problem for me to solve? Is reality such that whoever looks at it must see it as his personal problem? Can the helicopter have been materialized just so I could see the error of my ambition to solve a mechanical problem? Is this a persecution delusion? Like a portrait that stares directly at you wherever you stand?

Paradox 1:

With one hand I try my best to make the helicopter a success; with the other I hope that erroneous policies will reap their reward in a way that is clear enough to bring their reform. An impossible predicament, for if it succeeds in spite of the policies, they will not be recognized; or if it fails in spite of our efforts and its merits, these will not be recognized. The experiment is double; the answer ambiguous.

(For the records I should here note what has heretofore escaped being noted: The Gardenville group is almost completely annihilated and absorbed into the main aircraft group. Our blueprints are even removed. The machine shop absorbed into the larger experimental shop. The woodshop likewise. The pilots have other assignments.)

Paradox 2:

The answer to 1 is to walk off and leave it to its own working out. What then to do? On the one hand we have Bart and Tom with their determination to go on, eager to jump in and do it all over again. To follow their plan, we would manufacture the 47 and indulge in no experimental distraction, establishing in this way the solid foundation we have built so far, and reaching out into the new experiment of an industry keyed to the kind of problem the helicopter in service presents. My own instincts lead me to return to the womb, to *pre-*Gardenville, and make a simple, cheaper machine—or even to forget the helicopter altogether. This is perhaps not so much a paradox as a problem. It is, however, a paradox in the sense that we mutually perceive the handicaps imposed by a preexistent organization when we look at the floundering of Bell, yet we view our own "organization" (*i.e.,* Gardenville and Model 47) as exempt from the rule that specialization is death. But the quandary is real; insofar as other people are involved, other money, etc., we must crystallize out a tangible plan and structure.

Paradox 3:
    It might be "The horse eats in California, the ox digests in Maine."

    I was going to make a list of more paradoxes but I can't remember my first one. The real solution is to relax and let it run itself. This eager pursuit of a nonexistent answer is the error —and other Zen admonitions. How hard they are to apply. But at times I look up, see the sky, the peaceful aspect of nature— which is this struggle—and feel a surge of blissful joy. There is no rational answer. Does this mean there is no answer at all? Then there is no action to take—which must be false, for the strain of inaction is what is hardest to bear, what is causing "my nerves to shrink" [what the doctor said about my arms which I could not lift].
    Is there an answer not reached by tangible means? For such an answer are we to wait or to relax and let it come? Be careful, for the Zen books say we must struggle with our Koan, like a rat trying to escape from a terrier. The struggle causes the strain that breaks the chain and frees us.

June 24, 1947 (Evening)

The real point of these notes is to sharpen and extend self-consciousness. Therefore there is good reason for detail, especially of the thoughts induced by reality.

Now tonight, having been to the plant again today where I noticed very much the gloom of my Gardenville gang and with difficulty thrust the gloom away from myself, and having acute consciousness of the profound truth of the Hindu doctrines, I note about myself that I am but partially severed from the lures of reality.

I cannot yet feel a complete indifference to the helicopter. The urge to make it better, to fly it, to treat it right, still clings to me. Even if I got over the disease myself, I would be reinfected by contagion from my fellow people, who are all loyal to it.

You must acquire indifference to these things or go on until you do. About, say, credit for the helicopter, I am a little more advanced, for though I sometimes feel hurt that I am not credited with it, as soon as some credit does fall I realize its utter uselessness. In this I am not cynical. I think I can say I am truly indifferent.

And yet I feel more and more, by fragments and rare glimpses only, but nonetheless certain, the bliss of realization. To lean back on the "Thatness" as "the crow far from land trusts in the mast of the ship on which he sits." To be in a place and relax there, without the frantic urge to go on—I could stop the car now and sit without that compulsion to get where I'm supposed to be going. This is the flight one has invented the helicopter for, but even the bird is on the way, hence cannot enjoy his gift of flight.

In other words, for I have no desire to be obscure, we invent helicopters because we wish to fly. We wish to fly because we think it is the easy way to get somewhere. But we forget that the important thing is the *somewhere* and that transportation will never get us somewhere until we can learn that somewhere is a place where we stop wishing. So the problem of flight is solved by learning the "Thatness."

I find the "precepts of the Gurus," from *Tibetan Yoga and Secret Doctrines,* by W. Y. Evans-Wentz, very penetrating and sound. For a sample:

V. The ten things not to be avoided.

1. Ideas, being the radiance of the mind, are not to be avoided.
2. Thought forms, being the revelry of Reality, are not to be avoided.
3. Obscuring passions, being the means of reminding one of Divine Wisdom (which giveth deliverance from them), are not to be avoided. (If rightly used they enable one to taste life to the full and thereby reach disillusionment.)
4. Affluence, being the manure and water for spiritual growth, is not to be avoided.
5. Illness and tribulations, being teachers of piety, are not to be avoided.
6. Enemies and misfortune, being the means of inclining one to a religious career, are not to be avoided.
7. That which cometh of itself, being a divine gift, is not to be avoided.
8. Reason, being in every action the best friend, is not to be avoided.
9. Such devotional exercises of body and mind as one is capable of are not to be avoided.
10. The thought of helping others, however limited one's ability to help others may be, is not to be avoided.

Thursday (evening)

Carl stopped in in the evening. He asked about things and we finally got underway. Told him of my disinclination to get involved with the helicopter again. My interest now is philosophy, but I feel the need of Bart and Tom's brains for the problems ahead. My efforts to woo Bart to philosophy were not

successful. . . . Tom either. Carl expressed surprise. First time
I've heard you say you needed someone else. (But I have often
said how the past years have taught me that several heads are
better than one.) He said, "I see it more and more. You are not
interested in the helicopter." I said true, but I've found that
philosophy in itself is a liquid and has to be contained in
something. It can be poured in any shape of vessel. He said,
"You have not poured yourself into Bell. You remained yourself
and drops were scattered which people picked up." This shocked
me very much since I consider I leaned about as far as I could
without upsetting the boat. But his point can be allowed and
still not apply to the present. For my recent change has been to
realize that "this hand," which when a child I said "belongs not
to God but to me," is indeed not mine, and my childhood
declaration was wrong. (Not entirely, for the God in question
was the Sunday School God of my cousins.)

But again I say pour; I mean pour into a shape that is dictated
externally. In my case this was the helicopter as worked out by
the coming together of nature, the people, and myself. What I've
not accepted is the Bell shape because it would have been the
wrong shape. The new company idea has a shape which cannot
be as wrong as the Bell shape. In fact, if dictated by Tom and
Bart, it would be Gardenville. So Carl does me an injustice.

However, the value of what he says is that it is his direct
impression of my personality. He does not realize how hard I am
trying to get away from this limitation.

July 7, 1947

Some more ideas as a result of another tough day at the plant:
Bell the battleground of the spirit. Same problems as the
world. Bart replies, "I don't find the world so difficult to be
happy in." Well, I mean the world, including Russia.

While I worked on the transmission this morning, it was hard. I couldn't think what should be done. So I sat up straight. Do this at least, let come what will. By and by the idea did come, but regardless of consequence one can at least follow instructions.

The big trouble, or one of them, is that all these people (there are still 578 engineers) are unwilling to learn or to recognize there is something to learn. Therefore, one must wait. Suppose it's me that must learn. . . . So it is.

But not the same thing. I'm tempted to say they must learn about the helicopter. I can say this, must say it, or fall into the error of false modesty. But *I* must learn what I'm here and now trying to find the answer for.

The horse eats—the ox digests.

July 8, 1947

Some arguments to Bart yesterday about reasons for mentalism:

The glaring faults of science. We have been brought up to think we have an approximately true idea of the world, but our education is glaringly false for not only are we wrong in our facts, but our language for dealing with facts is wrong. True, we don't know what electricity is, hence cannot expect to know what hypnotism is. But what I find alarming is that we don't know hypnotism at all; *i.e.,* we should expect to know it (and metaphysics generally) in the same order as we know electricity.

July 9, 1947

Went to plant today.

We won our transmission.

Gloom in the sales department. The new dusting equipment worse than the old. Customers really mad. G. said, couldn't I make one, but I excused myself (I'm only a consultant). I felt highly oxygenated by the end of the day—although I'd taken no particular breathing exercises. This gave a feeling of elation. Am now making a special effort to be a female to my environment, embrace it, soak it up, smile upon it. And why not? Is it not my dream—or might I not be the God Vishnu in his boy form playing under the tree? To apologize for the vanity of this conceit would be truly insane, like Wentz's caution in his introduction to Tibetan book on how to change bodies—"that this is not for beginners." But truly the passage about Vishnu in the guise of the divine child—when he calls the hermit Markandeya a child, in Heinrich Zimmer's *Myths and Symbols in Indian Art and Civilization*—is as compelling as a story could be.

July 14, 1947

Should I pursue my duty in finishing the helicopter, instead of turning away from it? Should I interpret the pain in my arms, which is worse now, as a sign I am shirking the problem? I answer that I simply am not able at this point to step into this lion's den. Later, perhaps, but I must look for the treasure elsewhere first.

"Let go of the boat." A swimmer strains to cling to a powerful boat, hysterically afraid to let go lest he drown. Finally he releases his hold and immediately feels the violent tearing stop and floats calm and serene in the placid water. Am I still clinging to, shall we say, "logic"? Could I let go?

July 17, 1947 (New York)

Called Flettner—made appointment for dinner. When Flettner came I told him how his book *The Story of the Rotor* got me started on helicopters. [See Introduction.] He is a rather large, dignified man of sixty-one—very intelligent and simpatico. We had champagne cocktails. A small line was waiting for tables. When we went up, we asked for my table. I would have to wait, but not long. I told the headwaiter I had a distinguished guest. "So I see," he said. Flettner was that kind of man. He told me about

his latest ideas—for a large helicopter—but he could not disclose
them until he had the patents filed. The idea of taking him to
Bell appealed to me, especially when the friend whom he is
staying with explained that they did not want to start a new
company but make contacts with some well-established aircraft
company and "use the facilities." My thoughts kept turning over
the idea. What a joke it would be.

Bell would be happy; his dignity and prestige and the fact
that he had handled backers before would make him succeed
where I'd failed. He would be able to keep the engineers in line.
I called him Dr. Flettner but he said he preferred Mr. I said
don't fail to use the Dr. at Bell. I told the story of the engineer
who criticized my use of the word "wood-pile" in a memo
about conducting run-up tests on machines liable to fly apart.
Should say "barrier."

We had sirloin steak and Chambertin. Flettner still had the
recollection of scarce food under the Germans, the Russians. I
was in fine form and Flettner liked my jokes, which his friend
sometimes had to translate. My credo—money is not pure—it is
Wall Street money, beer money, coal money, and carries its
origin into the way it is spent. *Viz.*, Bendix, backed by Wall
Street, built a plant for production. The friend said that Bell
would be different. No, I said, that's aircraft money, and he got
the point. Advertising was very important. I told about my
decision to work on mechanical things instead of painting
because about the former one could get the answer from nature.
The friend said with such reasoning you would not be a painter.
But now I could see that this was not true. Even if nature says
yes, it still might not be accepted. The mind has to be ready for
it. "Suppose you had invented a flying saucer," I said. "You
would still not be able to convince people that they really
existed." "I believe," said Flettner, "that they are an optical
illusion."

I could see that his mind was immersed in the helicopter. He
was a much better person to carry on than I.

Since the idea that started me on helicopters was traceable to
Flettner's book, it was fitting that I should repay him. While the
issue might be in doubt (as to the advisability of his going with

Bell), it's my hunch that he would survive at least as long as Bell.

It was becoming increasingly clear to me how people pin themselves to the treadmill of their ambitions. Maybe mine is a hollow freedom, like that of a bachelor who laughs at his married friends who must report home to the little woman, but on the other hand I've given suck myself, and know what pleasure 'tis to nurse the child.

Did my exercises and went to bed. I woke up at five having just had a dream in which Dave asked me to make better dusting equipment. We'll give you your own group. You can build it "privately," he said. I answered, Why don't you build the helicopter "privately"? Dave winced. But I woke up with a feeling of great joy. I rolled around in the bed with a sense of physical and mental well-being. I was free, wonderfully free. Something about the decision to put Flettner into my place, something to do with handing back the jewel of thought I initially caught from the picture in his book—and with it the curse—had freed me.

Monday

Day at plant. A more intense feeling of weakness and liquidity than ever. This weakness is not the exact word. More a feeling of bonelessness—though it did not greatly affect my actions. Told Larry about Flettner and the large helicopter idea. He could not go into the merits of the idea. I strongly sensed his basic escape—nothing was said about the present situation, but there was the implication that he dare not even go into it.

When I got home I did my breathing exercises and felt that extreme desperation that would have made it possible for me to hold my breath until suffocation. My resolve did this. The waves of pain washed over me. I sat mute and accepting, praying for release. It was a sort of expiration. My desperation froze into a resolve firmly to refuse any further commitments.

Monday evening. Thought as the self-energized reality is a compelling idea. We may say in this connection that the so-called physical world is only the playground of ideas. Without ideas the world is nothing. Nothing happens to us unless we plan something. Against that plan reality creates itself by impinging. Thus today I found myself at Bell, very weary from doing nothing—because I had no plan, nothing really to do. The real world is the world of thought where plans are hatched. Having created the thought, we go out into the physical world.

August 1, 1947

Omitted exercises and breathing yesterday and this A.M. Cutting down on cigarettes does not affect appetite. Pain in arm was present in sufficient degree to interfere with normal activity. Kept remembering what I had written about pain being desirable, and not seeing anything desirable about it, even in retrospect. It kept me from thinking or feeling anything except itself.

On the way home from plant yesterday a small project party to celebrate J. D.'s leaving. Over whiskey, hot peppers, and onions, we reminisced on old Gardenville days. The warmth of pure human companionship; if anything, it flows more easily with these workmen than with my more educated friends. Such a soft warm thing it is—so full of true insight (as they asked me if I was still interested in the helicopter, about the coaxial), with our mutual dislike of the tyranny of organization, mutual joy in the incidents of helicopter history, the time the black dog got tangled up with the captive model, the time O. flew through the rotor (Tom told how he asked how much gas he had, told them to get behind the fence if anything went wrong, and they had stood, with mouths open, while pieces of rotor, bits of magnesium, flew around). To all of them and to me, these days will take on more luster with the passing of time—

an oasis of mutual working together in the desert of politics and falsehoods.

There is no contesting the absolute viewpoint of the humble. From this vantage point, the absurdities of situations, of people, show in sharp relief. How Dimitri put his arms over his head when the rotor came off the model. From the vantage of the slow rhythm of the spade, while the digger makes your grave, life is a parade of puppets and presumptuousness.

"Yoga of the Uncreated" [in *Tibetan Yoga and Secret Doctrines*]. Though I'm reading this for the third or fifth time, it is beginning to get heavy (I mean with meaning). I can realize that story which I now make up, of the man who began to think about thinking. He thought and he thought, but he did not think about thinking. He tried and he tried. Suddenly there was a puff and the man disappeared. No one knew, but a logician claimed that he had achieved success.

I realize what piddling I'm doing. There is work to be done.

"Existence"—the fact that existence is characterized by being other than nonexistence. The mind rebels at this. It is nonsense. Yet, think of a thing as existing—it is an "a" in a blank space. "What is 'a'?" "Other than blank." Therefore, blank is b. Therefore, a is surrounded by b. What properties has a? Well, "unity," a-ness (other than b-ness).

August 23, 1947

Last two days spent at plant. *The Cloud of Unknowing* had given me a new hold—especially the idea that the past is to be "trampled down in a cloud of forgetting"—which rules out the writing of journals. The emphasis on this principle (in *The Cloud*) is the purest and most scientific statement of the pure life, or of philosophy, of all-ness so far; there is no confusion, no inconsistency, no mixture of bromides and subtleties; it is all of a piece, and without compromise. This principle then, plus a quite remarkable feeling of wellness, which I believe is due to Hatha, floated me through these past two days with flying colors. Unfortunately, it leaves me in the quandary of not being able to write. All should be trampled down in a cloud of fogetting. The harm is done since I have not forgotten, however.

Several events testify to the success of the helicopter. Operators in Los Angeles had participated in battling a forest fire. One man completely surrounded by the fire would have perished, but the helicopter picked him up and took him to safety. A truckload of firefighters overturned on a mountain road. The helicopter rescued all of them, who I gather would have died in the fire; some were seriously injured. The same day seventy exhausted firefighters were replaced one by one with new men. Another story had it that an operator in Maine, had earned $28,000 in twenty days (dusting potatoes at $4 an acre). O. N., returned from Texas where three machines are on test with the Air Force, reported the machines doing very well and the instructors highly pleased with them, especially their performance and auto-rotation landings.

I also had a long talk with Strickler about general subjects I've been reading lately. His point of view is very much like my own. He wanted to find a rational or scientific way of expressing the laws of superconsciousness. I said that science is, by its very nature, limited to objective knowledge, whereas the method prescribed for the higher knowledge is subjective. To illustrate the limits of science, I instanced the criterion that you must be able to repeat an experiment and pointed out that this would exclude the experiment of telling a person a joke. To Strickler's suggestion that you could tell a different person for the second experiment, I said the point still holds; your audience may be all people, and the joke one that has no equal. (The experiment of presenting Picasso to the world cannot be repeated, and so on.) More generally, scientific knowledge hinged on identity. It is a way of knowing that considers only one thing at a time, the interval in Relativity. There may be other types of knowing. Science is essentially objective (it presumes that all knowledge is to reality as a map is to the place mapped). He seemed to ingest this type of reasoning and make intelligent comments. I wanted to suggest that he go out and feel the stick of Model 42 with the 48 rotor which has been subject to weaving, but we were interrupted. This would have given him an opportunity to *know directly* the stable rotor—and would have perhaps enlightened him a little on what constitutes making helicopters.

Thursday, T., R., and J. came in all upset because they could not eliminate weaving in the 48 rotor. I didn't want to help eliminate the weaving but I did want to help them solve it themselves, so I told about Charles Fort's stories of scientists who made announcements and then had to retract them because of being deceived by assistants. Also, if it had improved so far by my moving the center of gravity forward on the blade, they should continue to do this until they found the limit. This they did and it cured the trouble, and R. at least learned something, for he felt the stick before and after the fix and was aware of the difference. More and more it is appa.ent to me that it doesn't make much difference who it is; it's the extent to which they have experienced helicopters that counts.

Lately we had some mysterious cases of clutch slipping. I examined a clutch and found an interference that would have explained the slipping. The trouble was easy for me to find and correct. Lord knows how the system would have uncovered it. I imagined myself telling the story to Dave. He would have pulled the old bromide about, "Well, that's so-and-so's responsibility; one man can't do everything." This is the great fallacy, because it goes right up into top management and results in no management.

"For some mystics and gifted persons the omniscience of the supermind becomes conscious in the ego-form and we may accordingly explain clairvoyance, premonition, etc."

This is hardly fair, but it illustrates my point.

Whence cometh my carping? Perhaps these chaps would answer: this blandness you speak of is your own anxiety for things that don't exist. Nevertheless, there still is a point. *The Cloud* contrasts with all Hindu writing in evidencing an aliveness. The author describes the way to God like a bandit planning to rob a bank, excitedly, explicitly, economically—most Hindus are continually watering their stock with religious roughage, which I call spiricle.

Still I have not expressed my idea. Perhaps they are like playing a hose on a car, their flowing language engulfs us, make us gleam and glisten, then the sun dries the film of water and we are as dirty as before. What is necessary is soap or at least an all-over rubbing with a wet sponge to dislodge the coating of dust.

One has a right to grow critical because there are so many of these books now. Hocking (who writes the foreword) says:

> But the validities of these spiritual arts need to be subjected to a deeper and more objective analysis, capable of severely critical separation between irrelevant and essential factors.

(Compare, in *Vedanta and the Western World,* Huxley with his sharp, parried genuineness with the bland, nerveless discussion of the various Swamis.)

The possibility of a "scientific" explanation vanishing. Our governess is made out of gingerbread:

> Tale of little Johnny and his sister Kate who went for a walk with their tall governess, Miss Comstock. The children wanted to go through the woods and see once more the strange gingerbread house. Reluctantly the governess let them go. While they were playing in the gingerbread house Johnny broke the doorknob of the front door. For some reason he put it in his mouth. It had a delicious taste. The governess told him to stop but it was too late.
>
> Johnny was eating the doorknob. Kate tried to snatch it from him but got little satisfaction. So she went and ate the other doorknob. The children went wild pulling off the doorknobs; then they found the whole house was edible. Poor Miss Comstock. Only after they glutted themselves could she get them home. They were so full they would not eat their regular supper, so Miss Comstock put them to bed early.
>
> The next day they were forbidden to go to the wonderful gingerbread house in the woods. They cried and cried. After

their tears finally dried, Kate tried persuasion. She twisted
the button of Miss Comstock's sweater as she begged to go
to the wonderful house just once more. When the button
came off in her hand she put it to her mouth. It was
delicious peppermint! Miss Comstock was really disturbed
as little Kate grabbed another button. Miss Comstock tried
to get it out of her mouth. The child bit Miss Comstock's
finger—it was chocolate marshmallow. "Johnny," said Kate,
"Miss Comstock's made of candy, too!" So the children ate
Miss Comstock and went to live in the gingerbread house.

Scientific knowledge is limited by the requirement of being
able to repeat an experiment under laboratory conditions. This
has worked to the discredit of psychic phenomena generally.
Mediums don't always have 100 percent control of their
faculties—conditions are actually adverse—mediums become dry
or past their prime, etc. Certain experiments by their very
nature can't be repeated. The fact that a talent is fortuitous,
vagrant, unreliable, does not mean it is nonexistent or even due
to chance, but it does exclude it from "repetition under
laboratory conditions."

Hatha: Weight still down. Doing 30 breaths 8-32-16 instead
of Williamson's. Takes a lot of patience. Get my second wind at
about the 15th, from then on it's not difficult. Cat humps seem
now to be doing some good. I think a great deal of looking back
into the mind to see, yet it's not possible—or too difficult. First
we must have the calm. It seems as though I can feel the seven
centers of consciousness, yet I can equally well feel an extra one
at my mouth for instance, so this is illusion.

I'm thinking now of discontinuing the notes, principally due
to *The Cloud,* which stresses forgetting. Question then is, how to
forget. By not dwelling on the past? But the writing may
constitute a helpful dismissing—it is also a good discipline.
Certainly an ounce of realization, or of living the moment, is
worth pounds of rehash of the past. Yet, as said before, the light
sometimes comes in the realization of a meaning in past events
which was not apparent at the time.

Is there any system, other than Yoga, to accelerate
superconsciousness? *The Cloud* implies, like Zen, that there are

means for hurrying the growth. Painting? Yes, but my sudden glimpse has slipped back into the fog again. There is a possibility that in painting one can get a second wind, or perhaps, by painting several one after another, and with the pressure of time, so exhaust the conscious, the busybody planning mind, that one would be thrown back on one's instinct, onto the floor, like after the Providence helicopter crack-up.

August 30, 1947

Suppose we were discussing the existence of ether. We say ether is everywhere, transmitting waves at 186,000 mps. What contains the ether? Right away I'm stuck. We know from the Lorentz transformation that motion through the ether is meaningless. Why does it transmit at a finite velocity? If we can reason from the transmission of sound in air, we might say because its particles move at that speed. (With respect to what? With respect to each other. Then they have an air velocity.) But its particles must be without mass (for if they had mass and moved at that speed, mass would be infinite).

This is not the best thinking; it is supported thinking, supported by analogy with something we know, something finite. But still it's better than nothing.

The General Theory of Relativity tells us that rotation is absolute (explaining centrifugal force). Is gravitation (equivalent to negative rotation) absolute? Yes. With respect to what? With respect to the mass of all matter. Then if there were no other matter, there would be no centrifugal force and no gravitation.

Paradoxes (continued): A paradox can be pointed out in the frequent admonitions not to let thought dominate one, *e.g.,* how to avoid distractions in the Huxley article in *Vedanta and the Western World* where he quotes *The Cloud of Unknowing:*

. . . and try to look as it were over their shoulders seeking another thing, the which thing is God, enclosed in a cloud of unknowing.

In discussing one paradox I have brought up others, but let us return to the first one. Against these first references to *The Cloud* we have the ten necessary things from Wentz, *Tibetan Yoga and Secret Doctrines:*

(5) One needeth ability to fix the mind on a single thought even as a mother does who has lost her son.

Yet if the mother were endeavoring to reach God, the thought of her son would arise as a distraction.

The resolution of the paradox, which is more important than my exposition has made out, is, I suppose, that one must control thought. That is, be able to be like the mother who has lost her son, or to turn it off without a trace. But if one could turn it off, one would not be like the mother, and so forth. The same list says:

(6) Another necessary thing is to understand that there is no need of doing anything—even as a cowherd, etc.

But we have just been told:

(4) Again, one should comprehend that, as with a man dangerously wounded with an arrow, there is not a moment of time to be wasted.

I went to the doctor again about my arm this morning. When he asked if I was working too hard, I said not. I was perhaps suffering psychological "bends" due to removing myself from an atmosphere of nervous tension (pressure) to one of less tension.

He pulled the adhesive tape off my arm and in a relieved way explained that the tests showed I did not have tuberculosis.

The pure life. How unattainable, impossible, the pure life. Like an unstable airfoil in a strong wind, which will twist down, or up—but will not remain pointed in the right direction. I think now that we experience it, if we are lucky, only for a moment, such as at that moment when you realize that all is lost, and you give up. Then you suddenly feel it like a surge of power, but in a moment, after you again catch hold of yourself, it is gone.

Already (a few days ago) I found my scientific skepticism challenging the whole body of the occult and esoteric. Challenging it at least to bring it down to the same level with the data of science as reported by Charles Fort.

What's the use of all this? *The Cloud* plainly says, lose all the past in a cloud of forgetting, immerse all the now in the cloud of unknowing.

INNERSELF: Come now, you'll never get anywhere with this dole, this WPA service.

OUTER: What do you mean?

INNER: Give over all this placating of the sense of reason, this self-conscious apology. Give way to the pure reason, or to nonsense, or to love, or to anything to break that circularity.

OUTER: I'm doing all I can. The Tibetan Yoga says reason is not to be avoided since it's the best friend.

INNER: Not to be sought for either. Reason is a good comforter, but a poor advisor.

OUTER: What then to do?

INNER: Don't forget that those 1928 poems which you talk about so much were the end result of months of "abstract" or subconscious *practice,* remember?

OUTER: I do recall. I used to write page after page of gibberish. I called it Martian—and I never wrote *about* anything. I pulled out the threads of a sort of subconscious sweater.

INNER: It was thin stuff—just look back at these old notes and see how thin. You have much more fuel now. Why don't you wield the old axe? You're too careful. You know the formula, go to it.

OUTER: What formula? You mean grab hold of the mouse?

INNER: Yes, why not?

OUTER: I know what you mean, the desperation of one who hasn't time to think, grab the thing, but even then it was almost impossible, and so farfetched. Those efforts—to draw to phonograph records of Brahms, paint while playing Haydn, sealing wax, nothing can come of this. It would have to be about ten times better than it was.

INNER: Maybe you're thinking in terms of results. You didn't get enough paint on the brush, that's why it was thin. Besides, all that took place in a year or so. There's plenty of time—probe, delve, scrape that rear wall of the cave.

OUTER: What do you think about the helicopter?

INNER: Oh, forget all that; it's only a lump in your throat. Anyway, it's just blocking the natural flow you ought to have —like the problem you set yourself on friends; you keep trying to convert them. That isn't going to work, ever. Pass on; don't haggle over details.

OUTER: You sound like La Vie Bohème—expressionism and all that.

INNER: Oh no. I'm telling you to dig in, or fly, I don't care which, but stop just running your fingers over things.

September 3, 1947

A number of points came up with Brinton:

1. Our knowledge of matter is objective.

2. Our knowledge of force is subjective (objectively only its effects are observed).

Recent physics declares matter to be a form of force (or energy), not vice versa.

Therefore, through consciousness we can create physical effects.

The paradox does not abate. I hear myself advising, "Always keep hold of one branch while testing another (while climbing trees)"; i.e., trust no one. Yet this is just the opposite of what I've been telling myself. I must resign myself to God's will. I must accept the adventure of life. Too long have I been on guard. "In all other things use discretion, but in this, none."

Today Bart told me that he had walked into Larry with a
rewritten prospectus outlining a 100-ship program (per year)
with a unit price under $14,000. The schedule mentioned about
nine engineers, twenty-five machinists, welders, inspectors, and
metal men, twenty-five assemblers. Larry bought it all and
admitted that his experiment of doing it through the regular
engineering department had failed.

"I've tried it and now I know it won't work." According to
Bart it was a complete surrender. I said something about an
alcoholic who promises to go on the wagon and soon after Bart
said something that showed the old habits still linger.

There were more details—what to do about the 48. "Don't be
a quitter," said Larry, "they don't mind a flop—plenty of
airplanes are flops, but don't quit," and the Army is asking for
information on the convertible.

A. came in. He talked of the turmoil in the sales department.
The arguments thick and fast—Should they retrench? No, that
was defeatist. Crop duster tests at Batavia have not been
encouraging. It depends on the crop—cranberries, and potatoes
yes, orchards yes, other crops no. And arguments of policy. I
could see that there would have been no possible use in my
participating, any more than you can make water boil or glue
harden by anxious attendance. It was like filling an apparently
bottomless pit or pipe, and at last seeing the surface of the water
which signifies that the end is in sight, or hearing the sound of
picks after long arduous work on a rock tunnel.

Bart said they would henceforth manufacture no more bodies,
all bubbles, and that Larry was at least softening up on the
covered tail boom.

September 4, 1947

As I think of it now, I'm surprised that all this made so little difference to me. I was thinking of force = ma, E = mc², though I congratulated Bart and said if he got what he wanted, I'd come back to Buffalo and help or do research—whatever he wanted.

And now for other things—

Knowledge of matter is objective.
Knowledge of force is subjective.
Matter is unreal (by science's own determination).
Force is a component of energy, which is *real*.

What I'm getting at is to:

1. Explain that consciousness can create matter (with no logical impossibility—only a matter of degree).
2. Find what direction to take to do it. (What do we do to do it? How do we put things together?)

Yesterday I thought about the *Siddhis* [powers developed by the practice of Yoga]. What good are they? Proof that consciousness is more basic than matter? Why try to prove it? Faith will do the same. But there is doubt that it's true; proof is important. Maybe it's true because it can be true without upsetting the laws of science. (The psycho-physical theory and the principle that any moral law can interpenetrate the physical world; *i.e.*, the world, from the point of view of the elephants, can be said to be *for* the elephants.)

September 15, 1947

Talking to Brinton last night. He read his notes on hostility, its cure, etc. I tried to get interested in this approach, finally went over to my own present concern—the sin of nonaction. I outlined my predicament at Bell, how it motivated my interpretation of world problems, etc. Brinton thought hostility was the clue, but I persuaded him that this alone was not enough, using the image of the lighted match to see the glow of the moon in the mirror. Thus one must suppress one's own ego force (the light from the match) to make visible the light of the other person. Later I said the same technique can be used for drawing out the glow of the inner self. The meaning of the "razor's edge" is the path walled on one side by nonattachment, on the other by fear (being virtuous because of timidity).

Brinton thought this good. It was also, I believed, the real meaning of the golden mean. Graphically the golden mean is not just a halfway point between two extremes. It is rather an unstable point between two easier fallings off. On the one side we have self-styled virtue, on the other, actual sin.

My latest hallucination would be that life is planned so that each event has for each person a special intended significance. Those remarkable coincidences, which happen at just the right time and appear to be preordained for the sole purpose of creating a plan for us, are not just coincidences, but are so on purpose. I had been searching for a material that had the property of having a lower coefficient of static friction than its coefficient of dynamic friction. I had recently been investigating calcium stearate, and some samples were given to me by J. W. The calcium stearate had no mechanical properties (strength), so was not suitable. Had thought of trying Teflon, a fluorine compound used by the rocket group for a seal for high speed bearings running at very low temperatures, as in liquid oxygen, but inertia prevented my calling up to get it. At that moment N. walked in with a piece of Teflon that he had picked up in the shop where someone was making something out of it. This spurred me on and I made the telephone call to get more information. Then I went to the shop (feeling as though some ghostly parent were whispering the answer to help a child at an examination) but couldn't find the man who was making the stuff. As I walked through I saw N. (almost as though he had materialized in response to my wish). He told me where I could find more of the material. My plan was to make disks 1 5/8 inches in diameter, drill 3/4-inch holes in them, and use them for bearings in the tail rotor shaft. The mechanic using the material was making ball bearing adapters 2 inches in diameter and had as scrap two 1 7/8-inch disks which I could easily cut down to suit my purpose. There were thus three coincidences: first, N. bringing me the Teflon (which he had no idea I wanted); second, finding N. in the shop at the exact time I needed him; third, finding scrap pieces suitable for making what I wanted.

Now to the rational mind it is impossible that this should have occurred by intention. The way that it would be explained would be that the future is two-dimensional, hence the world plan can include the many futures which are required for the working out of the many plans that are simultaneously in operation. I feel somehow that the instance given in *Autobiography of a Yogi*, where the Yogi has a bowl of quicklime substituted for his bowl of milk, but feels no pain, whereas the person who played the trick is stricken with hideous gastric pains, has a bearing. The horse's frolic is the oxen's colic.

There is another explanation. Due to the "Dunne effect" we sense the future and are guided to intercept the coincidences. This raises the question of which includes which. Is the "Dunne effect" the basic one, of which the other is an example, or is there a prefabricated plan to which we more or less adhere? I rather feel that in the above there was more than the Dunne effect at work, since for example the size disks I needed was not one of arbitrary choice, a certain size was needed for the job I had in mind.

September 22, 1947
(in hospital, New York)

Here for a few days, owing to acute hemorrhoids and operation. Had hoped I would think and write during the convalescence but so far have been an absolute blank, not even successful in recording dreams. Reading *Black Hamlet* by Wulf Sachs.

For a long time I've been eager to find a doctor with whom I could discuss the many extraordinary and rejected data from Hinduism, theosophy, and metaphysics generally. The arms gave me a reason to consult doctors. But P. was a disappointment as were his colleagues. So I get to New York. I have an attack. In desperation I consult the nearest doctor, who is one who happens to live in the hotel.

It is all trash, and must be burnt in the fire.

My Yoga teacher disappointed me. Perhaps it was my piles, but his respected slogans irritated me. Yes, they are true, but why have I not benefited? Why, if that's the right way, has it not taken effect? Careless swagger, relax, don't try so hard. How can I try not to try? I told him I had this in my work, but not in my practice, but he did not say anything I didn't know already.

Yet one can never enter unless one has faith in one's Guru. I seem to lack faith in mine.

The last few days have been blank, except for a certain amount of pain. The drug Demerol is a wonderful thing; it gives one the relaxation one would take so long to achieve. Not having it I tried humming Aum—it worked. I relaxed like a baby, almost as well as with Demerol.

This ceaseless zigzag that gets nowhere—stop it.

Then the problem. So profound, so terrific; if it is as big as all this surely there is time, time to look about and tie one's shoelace. It is what I feared, one must walk into death and come back, and now I can't even remember my dreams, or suppress a desire for a cigarette. To say it's too difficult is sounding brass.

One has to pick up that limp thing, breathe life into it, and use it for a hammer.

September 26, 1947

Yoga of the Kathopanishad. Sri Krishna.

This book is certainly outstanding. I consider it better than the Vivekananda series—on par with *Tibetan Yoga and Secret Doctrines.*

The blazing eyes of the fierce beast that shine in the night—it is precisely between them that one takes aim and looses the shaft which is oneself, plunges oneself into the thick skull, into the marrow of density.

Then there was the time when you lit a camp fire to warm yourself—lit it on the forest floor of my soul—now the forest itself is on fire.

What is this consciousness? It is a wick that soaks up the fluid into which it is dipped. It is a long slither, a whip—in the hands of an expert it could slice off the cigarette that dangles from the lips of my lax attendant.

One has become accustomed to having the boundaries of misfortune become ever wider—but to experience the sudden expansion of the experience of bliss is altogether surprising and actually more convincing and humbling even than the view on a dark night of distant universes.

For problems to be completely solved there has to be the formal statement—it is not enough to do something. (Results are not enough.) My original reason for choosing machines as a career has not proved sound—even if it works, people have to believe it.

But above all and beneath all is the unstated fallacy of materialism—which is the belief in the nonexistence of the life force. Science or perhaps mathematics should be conscious of its own limits. Even as mathematics devises methods for dealing with ideas that cannot be visualized, so also can it devise methods for stating the limits of rationalism (just as it makes statements about infinity although it has never "been there").

The most basic characteristic of life is not growth and reproduction, as I was told in my college days, but sensitivity.

Further Notes on Organization versus Development:

When we say of an organism that its parts have the property of the whole, we are to some extent confronted with the limitations of sense-experience language. When we call a thing a part we do not actually make it a part; when we say that a part has a function, we are making an arbitrary classification. Thus we can take a segment of a root and put it in the earth; it responds by shooting forth a stem and leaves which move upward toward the sun; it shoots a further root down into the ground. Again certain species of earthworm, when cut in two, become two earthworms. Now if I take a stick, I may say that it has a middle and two ends, but if I break the stick in two, each piece has a middle and two ends. So in this case we are confronted with a situation where the sum of the parts is greater than the whole; for the stick has only two ends, but the sum of its parts has four ends.

We do not know the fundamental nature of life—perhaps that's why science is so slow to talk about it—but at least we can reason about the life principle and make observations. On the other hand, the immense growth of the physical sciences, and their extension into engineering projects, the automobile, the railroad, the airplane, the telephone, the radio, the movies, the microscope, telescope, and spectroscope have so thrust themselves upon us that we have been prone to give special sanctions to the principles under which they operate and to handicap ourselves with formulas of thinking that are really not at all applicable. So it comes about that the other sciences, outstripped by the mechanical ones, hope to aid themselves by the use of the tools that have been so successful in the physical sciences.

This is in essence the "evil" of materialism. It is entirely valid and good in the sphere for which it was invented, but

when it is applied outside this field we fall into error.
Communism and fascism are but the results of applying
materialism to the field of sociology and politics. The
application of materialistic concepts to the problems we have at
hand leads to similar errors. I like to think of the helicopter,
the latest child of the brain of man, forcing his parent to
extend his concept beyond the limits set
up by previous children of men's brains. The steam engine
engendered the theory of entropy which so influenced late
nineteenth- and early twentieth-century philosophy.

October 13, 1947

Hatha:
Went to New York October 7th and 8th. Saw Williamson. He
gave me new exercises: spinning the thread of Brahma, and the
first lesson in levitation, which was quite impressive. I have
dropped the other exercises, even breathing, confine myself to
Aum and this new one. Williamson said I'd been straining too
hard. Now I relax all the time, make no efforts. But I feel free.

Sir Jagadis Chandra Bose

> *The Motor Mechanisms of Plants* Longmans 1928
> *Growth and Tropic Movement of Plants* 1929
> *Plant Autographs and Their Revelations* 1927

It is a pleasure to read such simple, profound, and interesting
accounts. These books are very readable; by simple
straightforward work he establishes his momentous conclusions.
One wishes that more scientists would follow in his steps and
give up their passion for obfuscation.

In our Academy of Outcast Sciences we would include the confirmation and extension of this man's work. What else?

1. Confirm and extend Bose. Also present the story in film.

2. Horbiger, theory of the moon. Confirm Bellamy.

3. Theory of structure, organism, etc.

4. Study of ancient systems of thought, including astrology.

5. Study of psychic phenomena with a view to a constructive theory or science of the same.

6. Unbiased (?) confirmation of various startling pieces of so-called evidence for the paranormal: Sugrue (Cayce), Bennett, Cummins (it would be simple enough to verify the facts she avers).

7. Keep in close touch with nuclear and related physics.

8. Keep mulling over such mathematics as is available.

9. Track down Yogis both to confirm and obtain further information.

10. Compare and correlate similar evidence from diverse sciences: psychology, psychics, Yoga.

11. Fort technique. Track down and reveal the motives, etc., of the "qualified" skeptics. The Encyclopaedia Britannica has a scathing denial of psychic phenomena by Jastrow—find out what sort of man he is that he has so distorted the evidence. Similar denunciations are to be found elsewhere in the Encyclopaedia. Bacon theory, for example. Levi, for example.

12. Check up on the latest evidence about evolution, the problem of man's ancestry, as well as evolution of life in general.

13. Keep track of Ouspensky, Zen, Millikan, Michaelson, scientists who move over to the nonmaterialist camp. Assess their ability to contribute (to weed out the sentimentalists). Perhaps even enlist the services of many of them. This group would be balanced against those who have always been in the nonmaterialist camp, the esotericists. Then would arise the old political specter—a powerful minority of theosophists might steal the election—and cause the movement to lose its impartiality.

October 14, 1947

Ha Ha! Back in the sticky slime of intellectualism:

The Nature of the Physical World—Eddington
The Human Worth of Rigorous Thinking—Keyser
Probability—Fry
New Quantum Mechanics—Birtwistle
Textbook of Physiology—Howell
The Energy of Living Protoplasm—Lowe

The autobiography of a spy. To be written by myself.

Which will be an account of the strange life on earth of a man—who finds himself born in a strange country far from home, with a certain mission to perform. This mission is never clear to him, nor is he ever certain of his true allegiance—whether to be loyal to the oath he takes as citizen, or loyal to some deeper distant one that he has now almost forgotten, but of which his inner being constantly reminds him.

October 15, 1947

Spent most of yesterday at the plant. Flettner came. I was to
meet him in Larry's office, and he was going to tell about his
new ideas for a very large helicopter.

The idea proved to be the same one I have twice submitted
and often discussed: a very large rotor driven by small
propellers at the blade ends. It is not the same as the idea I
started on in 1929 because it recognizes the important factor of
size in its influence on helicopter design. For very large
machines the large diameter rotor and the mechanisms of
control become inordinately heavy. Essentially, "the idea" is to
recognize that for very large machines the design which places
the propellers at the ends of the blades, and in fact engines too,
is highly advantageous. It attains the desired rotor weight by
putting most of the machinery in the rotor. It keeps the control
forces in hand by using ailerons on the blades (as on airplanes)
instead of moving the whole blade. It solves the problem of
stability by keeping the weight near the rotor center.

Flettner's idea was the same, and he showed the drawings for
his recently filed patent, which consisted of some forty figures
showing configurations and design features, notably landing
wheels on the rotating part of the rotor with centrifugal weights
to retract them. We all listened—Larry, Dave, O., E., Bart, and
Tom. In every respect his ideas were in accord with my own
(though I told him later that I felt that his drawings indicated he
had overlooked the important consideration of torsional rigidity
in the blades, required to resist the large twisting moment
induced by the ailerons).

However, there was no question with me of rivalry. I had

hoped he had something newer and better. But as he didn't, it verified the conclusions I had already reached. My mission was to bring Bell someone who could make a large helicopter. [Flettner did not stay. As I heard it, he wanted the name of the company changed to "Flettner Helicopter Co."]

October 18, 1947

To continue the novel of the spy:

> His efforts to obtain a map from official sources proving futile, he is given one by an old man. His friends say the old man is known to them, that he is always offering this map, but that they themselves have dismissed it as a forgery. Meanwhile, the official geologists are working on a map. So far it has been made only for the inhabited regions, however.

Organism—we are drawn inevitably to concluding that the parts of the organism are identical to the whole, hence to each other, so that everything becomes identical to everything else. Problems of diverse aspects and locales have the same solution. This has been said by Indian philosophy. Perhaps we cannot afford to entertain so drastic a conclusion, but we can at least poke our heads out the door, and possibly step out into the garden and look back on the mansion of the mind in which we dwell—and see its limitations.

Any act of measurement or of statement involves the application of a known standard to something relatively unknown. This works only when the known standard is adequate. Sometimes it proves inadequate and the unknown becomes the standard. We have a portable crane which we use to lift boulders. Finally we come to a boulder so heavy that the portable crane tips itself over in attempting to dislodge it. Or we have a lever which we use to pry. We have also a fulcrum, but if the load becomes really heavy, the fulcrum moves more than the load.

I have seen a bulldozer pushing all the snow that covered the airport into an enormous pile. As the pile grew higher, footing for the bulldozer grew less secure. The pulpy snow which it pushed about so efficiently became a chaos of insecurity until at last it happened: the bulldozer became stuck in the great slushy morass. The operator finally gave up and told his foreman. The latter, who was an old hand, got in and, using the bulldozer's retracting plow, reversed its function, so that instead of lifting and pushing the snow, it lifted the bulldozer—and so extricated itself.

This is man's limitation—that he can lift only such loads as will not displace his biological foundation. But if he gets stuck, he can still get out—for load and fulcrum can reverse—and man, the inner, can extricate man, the outer, by using his own graspers and stealers to lift himself instead of the burden. This is what we know as the religious quest.

Another paradox:

All Yoga books tell us the importance of controlling the senses. Or of maintaining a consciousness of what one is doing while doing it. Of keeping the self poised and balanced while standing on the furiously swaying chariot of the body, like a man keeping his balance on the shaking narrow platforms they have in amusement parks.

And yet all my experiences of the superstate have occurred either during or just after an out-of-body experience when the senses were so overpowering as to sweep one off one's rational balance.

This happened on both occasions when helicopters were wrecked with loss of life—"Sitting down in the chair" and "Giving in to the hound of heaven," which I've already recounted. But here is another.

In 1932 when I went with my brother Chris to Switzerland, he took me to a hotel on the Jungfraujoch where we went skiing. I found the skiing dull and one day inquired of the guide whether we could make the ascent of the Jungfrau. The guide said it could be arranged, and the next day we set forth. I gathered that it was a rather easy ascent which was part of the regular tourist itinerary. (I had never been interested in mountain climbing but this time the mountain was right there. I was curious for a taste.)

As we prepared to set forth, the valley was quite hot. It was May, we had gone for the spring snow. I was wearing a light open-weave sweater. I asked the guide if it was sufficient clothing. Either he didn't understand or didn't know, but he said it was. So we set forth. We climbed some distance on skis, then removed them and put on crampons, spikes strapped to the shoes to enable one to climb on the ice. After the long snow-covered slope up which we'd come on skis, we were confronted by a snowdrift some twenty feet high which was even steeper than perpendicular. Somehow the guide conquered it and with the help of the rope the rest ascended. I took movies as I struggled up. Once over this, we crossed a gently inclining plateau and came to the foot of the long steep slope of the peak, covered with hard ice and devoid of any foothold. To progress it was necessary for the guide to cut steps with his ice pick, which took a long time. The rest of us waited while he cut them.

I began to get cold. As we ascended the wind blew stronger and stronger, the air colder. It cut through my open mesh sweater. I began to shiver. I flung my arms about to keep up circulation. The rest of the party were properly clothed, with windbreakers, etc., so I suffered alone. I shivered violently. So violent were my sensations that I could retain no self-control. I cried out and swore and yelled. The others in the party were sympathetic but had their own troubles—a slip and we'd all slide down. This went on for an hour or so. Before we got to the top I was practically hysterical, though, I will admit, entirely conscious. I just didn't care. The swearing and yelling afforded a kind of relief, so I was entitled to it. On the peak it was still cold but I could jump about to keep warm. The guide gave me a sip of some sweet cherry brandy. I wrote a postcard to Priscilla.

We made the descent. I felt elated. I tore off the rope and ran down the hill, disregarding entirely the carefully cut steps, and the remonstrances of the rest of the party. I was no longer cold, my body was an excellent device, and perfectly capable of carrying me down this silly mountain. When we got to the point where we'd left our skis, I pointed them straight down—sat on my tail and zoomed down the mountainside, followed by a minor avalanche.

I am still repeating it: superconsciousness is produced by the tearing of the mind from its secure foundations by the force of the body. Racking pain, hideous tragedy, pleasure beyond the boundaries legalized by "mind"—all do this. Mind and body float in the ocean like seaweed dislodged by the storm.

Fable:

I have heard tell of a piano which was well-behaved and extremely sedate. It sat in the parlor of a great house and its gleaming black surface reflected the life of the people who lived there. At times great musicians would come. Their tortured hands would fly over its keys and the piano would resound with marvelous reverberation. All this was very pleasing to the piano, and it reveled in such skillful caresses, and enjoyed its own resonant tones. One day there came to that house a master. He made no elaborate stir when he sat down and there was no rustle of dresses and whispered remarks from an audience. He came in the twilight and his fingers ran without effort over the keys. The piano was pleased, and settled back to be entertained by its own reverberations.

But subtly, slowly, a strange stirring began to occur, for this time the music was more beautiful than it had ever been before. The dignified poise which the piano was accustomed to preserve soaked up the persuasive force of the music, dissolved, and grew limp. The piano felt itself begin to move, to sway to its own music, and as the fingers moved over the keyboard in the dim light, it felt itself one with its own chords and its swaying became a dance, and its dance a flight; piano and music and musician became one floating pulsing thing—it thrashed and it screamed and it soared until finally it emptied itself of all its crisp edginess and lay on the floor like spinach. The musician vanished; the long night passed, and when morning came the piano pulled itself together back to its former propriety. But it always remembered its twilight cavorting, and when others played on its gleaming ivory keys, now tinted faintly with brown, it swayed just a little and sensed more feeling in its rich tones.

October 24, 1947

We have had our farewell to Buffalo party. Larry Bell came. Everything went off beautifully, the food delicious, the music, the decor, the company. We got home after three, though some witnesses state it was four.

November 12, 1947 (Washington)

Spent yesterday 2–10 at Library of Congress.

Subjects: Jung—sleep—Bose—with a side excursion to see my article in *Interavia*—no success—but I stumbled on July issue of *General Psychology* which had an article by Daly King on consciousness.

Jung is a great man—one of the great minds of our time. What a contrast with, say, Kleitman, who had a book on sleep with a bibliography of 1,434 items. It makes me so mad. In this confused hodgepodge of references, he reigned, understanding nothing, and all at Rockefeller expense. There was not even a reference to Jung or Yoga, just a number of things like an attempt to induce hibernation in a muskrat:

11:00 A.M.   Muskrat dipped in cold brine.
11:20 A.M.   Muskrat removed—violent shivering.
11:25 A.M.   Muskrat dipped in cold brine.
11:30 A.M.   Muskrat removed—violent shivering and so on
                about 10 times.
3:00 P.M.   Muskrat removed. Muskrat dead—and so on.

In the final chapter, having cited all the theories of sleep (due to change in the blood, sugar content, nerves, etc.), he starts to tell his own theory.

After all, he says, it's not a matter of explaining sleep but explaining being awake—and thus brilliantly he closes the book. Oh, my God!

In King, too, we sense this blind devotion to the bias of science—a sort of special grace attached to the measurement of things and a scorn of the subjective approach, as though all measurement were not subjective.

What they fail to appreciate is Jung's empiricism; he doesn't claim to know what he's dealing with, but in his digging he finds shapes, shapes that are real because they recur and can be usefully applied. Like the shapes the physicists find in the atom, the shapes are not projections of common sense (billiard balls); they are patterns of action that are unknowable directly but can be identified by their effects (quantum theory in general).

Jung's definition of archetypes. His true understanding of religion—Catholicism versus Protestantism—of the German mind, of ancient symbols, alchemy, of revelation in dreams. (His lecture at Yale I read in its entirety.)

Bose's failure to get his work published in scientific journals was brought about by only one or two men—Sanderson and another physiologist. One must not exaggerate the idea of religious persecution of original ideas. There were plenty of English scientists who appreciated Bose—especially in the enthusiasm of the moment after his lecture.

[My lecture on helicopter stability in 1941 in New York was greeted with great applause and enthusiasm. It was never published because of a suspicious train of accidents. The stuffed shirt who had charge of reviewing these papers had said the year before that my work was questionable. This time he said nothing whatever about it, on the grounds that it contained "matter of value to the enemy," for we had just gone to war.]

But beside the particular rebuffs accorded Bose and which he overcame by sheer fight, there was and is a general smugness. The wound he made in the body of smugness has healed—people speak of him as queer. No one carries on his work, and why?

Because to a great extent science is the knowledge of little men—it survives only if it can be duplicated by the clumsy ones. An exception I suppose is physics. Will have more to say after I've been to the Institute of Advanced Stuffiness at Princeton.

Above the restaurant opposite the Library was an office for rent. How simple. I could establish my "Academy of Outcast Sciences" right here—with the whole Library of Congress to draw upon.

EPILOGUE

[After I left Bell my notes were devoted to other subjects, such as psychoanalysis. However, I made occasional visits to Bell and the following note is significant for it was because of Bart's leadership that the Bell helicopter gained and retained its leadership in the field.]

October 4, 1948

O. out, Bart in.

Bart's stature grows to heroic proportions. He won his present spurs. What happened was this. All of O's projects collapsed. The Trainer program and others failed to win an Army contract. Bart's work on the 48 made it a good ship. The enthusiasm when he got it flying on schedule (the Army accepted it, and he'd done it at the cost he said he would) was evidently unbounded.

All the rest of the people are looking up with Bart in the saddle. Carl gets his cooperation. The service department is no longer at dagger's point with engineering. Now all that remains is production. Bart and Tom have been getting into this and doing good work.

[In 1948 I married Ruth Forbes and, with her as a partner, began a new life devoted to my interest in those aspects of existence not recognized by science. This in turn led to a restudy of science itself and then to the development of the paradigm described in my two books, *The Reflexive Universe* and *The Geometry of Meaning.*]

INDEX

About the Author

ARTHUR M. YOUNG, inventor of the Bell helicopter, graduated in mathematics from Princeton University in 1927. In the thirties he engaged in private research on the helicopter and in 1941 he assigned his patents to Bell Aircraft and worked with Bell to develop the production prototype. In 1952 he set up the Foundation for the Study of Consciousness, superseded by the Institute for the Study of Consciousness, located in Berkeley, California, and dedicated to the interpretation of science to include life and consciousness. Arthur Young is the author of *The Reflexive Universe* and *The Geometry of Meaning*.